A Future
for
American Evangelicalism

A Future
for
American Evangelicalism

Commitment, Openness, and Conversation

HAROLD HEIE

Foreword by Randall Balmer

WIPF & STOCK · Eugene, Oregon

A FUTURE FOR AMERICAN EVANGELICALISM
Commitment, Openness, and Conversation

Copyright © 2015 Harold Heie. All rights reserved. Except for brief quotations in critical publications or reviews, no part of this book may be reproduced in any manner without prior written permission from the publisher. Write: Permissions, Wipf and Stock Publishers, 199 W. 8th Ave., Suite 3, Eugene, OR 97401.

Wipf & Stock
An Imprint of Wipf and Stock Publishers
199 W. 8th Ave., Suite 3
Eugene, OR 97401

www.wipfandstock.com

ISBN 13: 978-1-4982-0878-9

Manufactured in the U.S.A.   03/11/2015

Dedicated to Stan Gaede,
a friend for many years who models that rare combination of
commitment and openness.

Contents

Foreword by Randall Balmer | ix
Preface | xi
Acknowledgments | xv

1 Introduction: American Evangelicalism and the Broader Christian Tradition | 1
2 Continuing the Conversation | 21
3 Evangelicalism and the Exclusivity of Christianity | 24
4 Evangelicalism and the Modern Study of Scripture | 35
5 Evangelicalism and Morality | 51
6 Evangelicalism and Politics | 68
7 Evangelicalism and Scientific Models of Humanity and Cosmic and Human Origins | 92
8 Evangelicalism and Higher Education | 108
9 The Future of American Evangelicalism | 135

Bibliography | 145
Contributors | 151

Foreword

For me, one of the striking characteristics of the gospels is the amount of time that Jesus spends listening to others and communicating quietly with them. Think of Zacchaeus, the woman caught in adultery, and countless others who came to him for healing. Jesus engaged them, looked them in the eye, and heard what they had to say.

For many years now, Harold Heie has exemplified this model of listening—what he calls the combination of commitment and openness. No one would question Jesus' commitment to the radical ethic of love that characterizes the gospels, but no one doubted his receptivity to others. We live in a time of prepackaged ideas and polarized ideologies: red and blue, Republican and Democratic, the *Wall Street Journal* and the *New Republic*, conservative and liberal. Sadly, this dualism has also infected evangelicalism, where the faithful are asked to choose sides on the theological, social, and political issues of the day.

Harold Heie summons us to a different, more elevated level of discourse, one in which individuals are willing to articulate their convictions without fear of disdain or censure or reprisal, one in which others listen carefully and critically and are willing to withhold judgment—at least until they understand perspectives other than their own.

This volume represents a sample of the kind of respectful conversation that Harold has encouraged for a very long time. The voices in this conversation do not agree with one another, not by

Foreword

any means. But they have committed themselves to dialogue. The conversation in these pages is marked less by megaphonic declarations than by careful, reasoned, irenic discourse. Similarly, no reader will agree with everything in these pages, but that is precisely the point. Evangelicals do not speak with one voice; they speak with many voices.

Harold Heie calls evangelicals to both commitment and openness. The danger of commitment without openness is dogmatism, and the peril of openness without commitment is relativism. Together, however, one tempering the other, evangelicals can navigate the straits between Scylla and Charybdis.

Randall Balmer

Preface

I never tire of sharing the perspective on "religious maturity" that was proposed by the late Ian Barbour, a renowned scholar who worked at the interface between science and religion:

> It is by no means easy to hold beliefs for which you would be willing to die, and yet to remain open to new insights; but it is precisely such a combination of commitment and inquiry that constitutes religious maturity.[1]

These words are the bedrock for this book. They point to two poles: commitment and openness. My experience suggests that many people inhabit one of these poles; very few embrace both. My overarching thesis is that the variegated movement within America known as "Evangelicalism" has a bright future if, and only if, those who consider themselves to be evangelicals embrace this rare combination of commitment and openness.

COMMITMENT

I admire those who are deeply committed to their beliefs, and I aspire to always be one of them. Such people know what they believe and are willing and able to articulate their beliefs with deep conviction. Many hold to their beliefs with such tenacity that they would be willing to die for them.

---

1. Barbour, *Myths, Models, and Paradigms*, 138.

Preface

But much destruction has been wrought by some of those who exclusively inhabit this pole. As C. S. Lewis has observed, "Those who are readiest to die for a cause may easily become those who are readiest to kill for it."[2] Such people are not willing to entertain the possibility that they could be wrong about some of their beliefs. As a result, their lack of openness to considering the contrary beliefs of those who disagree with them can too easily lead to fanaticism or even terrorism. Commitment needs to be accompanied by openness.

OPENNESS

I also admire those who are open to carefully considering the views of those who do not share their beliefs, and I aspire to always be one of them.

But some who display such openness to others' beliefs are hesitant to express their own beliefs with clarity and conviction. They too easily fall into the relativist trap of concluding that "you have your beliefs, I have mine," such that there is not much point in engaging one another about our disagreements. The reigning epistemological stance of many in our day and age is "whatever," which negates the possibility that there may be some Truth about the matter at hand, and we should engage one another in an attempt to get closer to that Truth. So, openness without commitment is also inadequate. What is needed is that rare combination of commitment and openness. It ought to be both-and, not ether-or.

My suggestion that the commitment pole must be accompanied by the openness pole may lead a number of readers to conclude that I am "soft on the Truth." Not at all! It is merely my acknowledgment that I am on a pilgrimage toward a better understanding of Truth, which is far removed from a denial of Truth. In fact, it is a sign of my utmost seriousness about the Truth. Whatever the issue at hand, I believe that there is some Truth about the issue that God fully knows. But I am not God. As a finite, fallible,

---

2. Lewis, *Reflections on the Psalms*, 28.

Preface

and sinful human being, I do not have a "God's eye" view of the issue at hand. I only "see through a glass darkly" (1 Cor 13:12). The truth that I have come to believe may not be the same as the Truth as God knows it. Therefore, I need to talk to those who have different beliefs about the Truth relative to the issue, opening up the possibility that we can both arrive at an improved understanding of that Truth, which leads me to my core commitment to conversation.

CONVERSATION

My overall purpose in writing this book is to attempt to present a compelling case for my belief that the primary telltale sign of a vibrant American Evangelicalism in the future will be the practice of evangelicals creating welcoming spaces for respectful conversation with those who disagree with them (among evangelicals, within broader Christian circles, and in the larger culture). In such safe spaces, conversation partners should be able to express their beliefs with deep conviction and, at the same time, show that they are open to listening to the contrary views of others and respectfully talking about their disagreements with the goal of gaining a better mutual understanding of Truth.

Given the great diversity in belief and practices across the various streams of the evangelical movement, my dream for such respectful conversations about disagreements will only be possible if we, as evangelicals, make a commitment to exercising the Christian virtues of humility, patience, courage, and especially love, since providing a welcoming space for someone to disagree with you and then engaging that person in respectful conversation is a deep expression of love for that person, to which Jesus calls all of us who aspire to be his followers.

Preface

GOD'S PROJECT OF RECONCILIATION

The pages that follow report on the results of an electronic conversation (eCircle) that I hosted on my website (www.respectfulconversation.net) on the topic of "American Evangelicalism," to which twenty-six evangelical scholars, working out of a variety of evangelical traditions, posted brief position papers on eight sub-topics.

If you read though the original postings on my website in addition to the pages that follow, I believe you will see compelling evidence that these scholars engaged one another in conversation with deep respect in the midst of their disagreements, modeling the rare combination of commitment and openness that I call for in these pages.

And a marvelous by-product of this "respectful conversation" is that out of this plethora of varied voices, a theme appears to emerge—participation in God's Project of Reconciliation may be the "working Center" that can hold evangelicals together in the midst of great diversity in beliefs and ecclesiastical practices.

Acknowledgments

I first extend a deep word of thanks to my twenty-six regular contributors to my online conversation. Despite their own very busy schedules, these contributors faithfully posted their position papers every month for eight months. I personally benefited a great deal from reading their thoughtful and insightful postings. They are the people who made this project work.

I also thank the readers of my eCircle who submitted thoughtful comments on the postings of our contributors. Their respectful comments added richness to our conversation.

A special word of thanks goes to Rob Barrett, Director of Fellows and Scholarship for The Colossian Forum (TCF), and to Michael Gulker, President of TCF, for their steadfast support of this project. Rob served with distinction as co-moderator of the eCircle by formulating the compelling "leading questions" that were the springboard for each monthly conversation. It was under Michael's leadership that TCF agreed to pay the costs associated with managing my website during the eight months of the conversation and for advertising this conversation in selected venues. This project would not have happened if it were not for this generous financial support, for which I am extremely grateful. It is an honor for me to serve as a TCF Senior Fellow, since their mission to create a "safe place" that "facilitates dialogue on divisive issues within the church" comports so well with my commitment to facilitate respectful conversations about contentious issues.[1]

---

1. "All Things Hold Together in Christ," *The Colossian Forum*, 2015, http://

Acknowledgments

In addition to TCF, two other organizations co-sponsored the eCircle: the Center for Faith and Inquiry (CFI) at Gordon College and Eastern University. A special word of thanks goes to my friends at these organizations who made this happen: Tal Howard, Director of the CFI, and Kenton Sparks, former Provost at Eastern University.

Brian Workman, co-owner of the Five Espressos web design and development company, served with distinction as my web manager leading up to and during the eight-month eCircle. I thank Brian for the extremely competent, efficient, and gracious manner in which he managed my website.

I thank Beth DeLeeuw, who served with distinction as my Administrative Assistant at Northwestern College in the 1980s, and who was immensely helpful in formatting portions of this book manuscript.

I also thank Matthew Wimer, Laura Poncy, and Alex Fus of Wipf & Stock Publishers for the professional, efficient, and gracious way in which they brought this book to publication.

My deep commitment to fostering respectful conversations among those who disagree with one another has been deeply informed by the example of friends who have modeled such commitment in their lives. Since we were colleagues on the faculty of Gordon College in the late 1970s, Stan Gaede has been one such special friend. He models beautifully that rare combination of being deeply committed to his own beliefs at the same time that he is open to empathetically listening to and engaging in respectful conversations with those who disagree with him. Although Stan may find much to disagree with in the views expressed in this book, I dedicate this book to him because he will be happy to say, "Let's talk."

Finally, I want to express my deep appreciation and love to my wife, Pat. Many years ago when I was absorbed by a sense of self-importance outside our home, Pat modeled for me by her splendid example that the real heroes of the Christian faith are not necessarily those on public display, but rather those who in the

---

www.colossianforum.org.

Acknowledgments

daily routines of life, without any fanfare, exhibit the fruits of the spirit one minute at a time: love, joy, peace, patience, kindness, generosity, faithfulness, gentleness, and self-control.

1

Introduction

American Evangelicalism and the Broader Christian Tradition

DIVERSITY AS A HALLMARK OF AMERICAN EVANGELICALISM AS A MOVEMENT

Evangelicalism is a worldwide movement, with some of its most robust streams presently flourishing in the global South. My project is limited to consideration of the evangelical movement in America.

Even within the American context, many of our contributors join the chorus of Christian scholars who note the difficulty, if not impossibility, of unambiguously defining "evangelical" or Evangelicalism.[1] Amos Yong observes that "the question of *What is Evangelicalism?* rages on," while Vincent Bacote suggests, "'evangelical,' like 'postmodern,' can mean both everything and nothing." Corwin Smidt says that "it is not self-evident just to what one is

---

1. See the bibliography for a portion of the voluminous literature on the history of Evangelicalism, the contours of evangelical theology and the role of Evangelicalism in public life.

referring when the terms 'evangelical' or 'Evangelicalism' are used." John Wilson asserts that "we find in the history of Evangelicalism no single stance or attitude that can be called definitive for this particular stream of the faith." Likewise, Peter Enns says that "defining 'Evangelicalism' in America is like trying to hit a moving target," suggesting that when we try "to capture the essence of what Evangelicalism means," we "often work off of impressions based on our own experiences."

This ambiguity is not surprising, given the multiple roots of those who situate themselves as evangelicals, including those who trace their beliefs to the tenets of the Protestant Reformation; those who trace their expression of the Christian faith back to the revivalist movements in eighteenth-century America; those who, like me, are the descendants of Pietist immigrants to America from Scandinavia and Germany; those who associate Evangelicalism with particular institutions or leaders; those who trace their evangelical lineage to the fundamentalist movement that was a reaction to Protestant Liberalism and Modernism; and those who associate with the neo-evangelical movement that was a reaction to fundamentalism.

Consistent with these diverse streams, a number of our contributors suggest that Evangelicalism should be considered to be a "movement" that transcends particular Christian traditions or denominations. For example, as John Franke explains:

> I have always had the sense that Evangelicalism is more like a particular movement within the larger history of the Church and the churches, rather than something more central. I have never understood the evangelical tradition as something distinct from other traditions but rather as a general movement within various traditions. So we see Presbyterians, Lutherans, Episcopalians, Anabaptists, Baptists, Pentecostals, etc., who also identify as evangelicals.

Viewing Evangelicalism as a movement in this way leads Franke to point us to the "diversity" in evangelical belief and practice: Evangelicalism is "a movement that crosses theological,

Introduction

denominational, confessional, and ideological boundaries. In so doing, it manifests diversity that has been an inherent part of the North American evangelical movement since its beginnings."

Kyle Roberts also notes the "perplexingly variegated concoction of Christians" who are evangelicals, and he attributes this diversity to "the renewal and reformist impulses of the various evangelical streams," which he notes with approval, saying that he resonates "in particular with Amos Yong and John Franke when they emphasize [these] . . . impulses" in their postings.

Consistent with the diversity in Evangelicalism pointed to by John Franke, Kyle Roberts suggests that "perhaps it's time we think of 'evangelical' as an adjective—a qualifier nuancing a more central identity: Christian or *Christ Follower.*"

Echoing Peter Enns' suggestion that when someone tries to capture the essence of what Evangelicalism means, he or she often works off of impressions based on personal experiences, Jeannine Brown observes that a "theme that emerged in the [electronic] conversation is that of social and theological location," adding that "if Evangelicalism is a *located* stream within the Christian tradition, then an important invitation involves acknowledging that location with the broader Christian tradition." Brown concludes that such acknowledgement of the "locatedness" of our expression of evangelical Christian faith could be the basis for a helpful dose of humility.

RESPONSES TO THE DIVERSITY WITHIN EVANGELICALISM

If we acknowledge the diversity within Evangelicalism, it is equally clear that evangelicals disagree on how to respond to that diversity. Some seek to eliminate Evangelicalism's diversity, while others embrace it.

John Franke notes the tendency of many evangelicals to seek to eliminate diversity in evangelical belief and practice:

A Future for American Evangelicalism

While the evangelical movement has been characterized by a rich ecumenical diversity, this does not mean that evangelicals are comfortable with this plurality. For the most part they are not. Instead, they tend to be committed to establishing the one true faith over against other versions. They pursue the one true way to be a Christian, the one right way to read the Bible, the one true system of doctrine, the one right set of practices.

This aversion to diversity on the part of some evangelicals has had two interrelated results. It has led to an attempt to establish "limits" or to tightly define "boundaries" beyond which a given belief or practice is unacceptable for an evangelical. This suggests a "policing" role. Kyle Roberts asserts that what has "empowered" that policing tendency is the "false narrative of a single 'Evangelicalism,'" adding that greater appreciation for the Pietist and Pentecostal streams could "disabuse people" of this false narrative, possibly leading to "a better shot at shaking free of the police," which we will discuss at length later.

Of course, the debate as to what these boundaries are is messy at best, leading to the second result of an aversion to diversity, as stated by Franke: "In their collective search [for the one true set of beliefs and practices] different groups have come up with alternative and competing conclusions. This has spawned a seemingly endless series of contentious and ill-tempered debates concerning theology, hermeneutics, ethics, and church practices."

The sad result, according to Franke, is conflict and divisiveness within Evangelicalism. As he explains, "These conflicts have produced a divisive and contentious spirit among many evangelicals that has significantly compromised our witness to the gospel."

Vincent Bacote does not paint so dire a picture of present-day Evangelicalism. He acknowledges the diversity, but he perceives a certain respect among those who hold to different beliefs and practices: "Part of the strength of Evangelicalism is the fact that it is a conservative Christian ecumenical movement that brings

Introduction

together a wide range of denominations *while respecting (sometimes) differences in doctrinal emphasis and ecclesial practice.*"[2]

Whatever level of divisiveness we perceive within present-day Evangelicalism caused by such an aversion to diversity, Franke points us to another possible response to that diversity. It is something to be embraced as "the blessing and intention of God." He elaborates:

> The diversity of biblical, theological, and confessional perspectives in Evangelicalism and the broader Christian tradition are a necessary and appropriate manifestation of the church. This is because no single linguistic context or interpretive community is able to bear fully adequate witness to the truth of the living God.

I personally embrace Franke's view of the diversity within Evangelicalism as a gift from God, based on my own experience. In over-simplified terms, my in-depth immersion in three different streams of Evangelicalism has taught me to respect the unique emphases of each stream as capturing a portion—but not the entirety—of what Franke calls "the truth of the living God." In my Pietistic Lutheran upbringing, I learned to value deeply-felt religious experience. Within the Reformed tradition, I learned to value the life of the mind. Within the Anabaptist tradition, I learned the importance of living out what you say you believe and feel. Yet I also saw firsthand some extreme attempts to marginalize those outside the given stream—falsely equating Pietism with mindless emotionalism, or the Reformed tradition with arid intellectualism, or the Anabaptist tradition with uninformed activism. Such extreme views fail to realize that all of these expressions of the Christian faith make an important contribution to a comprehensive understanding of what it means to be a "whole Christian person," giving expression to the cognitive, affective, and volitional dimensions of personhood.

My enthusiasm in embracing Evangelicalism's diversity as a gift from God is foundational to the message of this book. It is

2. Italics mine.

because I believe that those believers embedded in different streams of Evangelicalism have much to contribute to a full understanding of the Christian faith that I want each evangelical to express his or her commitments with clarity and deep conviction. At the same time, I want each evangelical to stay open to respectfully listening to and talking with those evangelicals who hold to differing beliefs and practices—the goal being that by learning from the best of each stream of Evangelicalism, we can gain a better understanding of the Truth as only God fully knows it.

THE POLICING TENDENCY FROM BOTH ENDS OF THE SPECTRUM

Before I propose a strategy to facilitate respectful conversation among those embedded in different streams of Evangelicalism who, like me, wish to maximize the potential of the gift of diversity, I will say just a few words about the legitimate concerns of those evangelicals who worry about the diversity of evangelical belief, whether from the "right" or from the "left," and who, therefore, want to tightly define and police the boundaries of acceptable evangelical belief and practice.

There are some developments in theology that are of great concern to many traditional evangelicals. These include current debates about the historicity of Adam and Eve and related issues concerning origins, theories of atonement that call into question the traditional evangelical view of the "substitutionary sacrifice of Jesus Christ," and debates about the "modern study of Scripture," the exclusivity of Christianity, and human sexuality.[3] A legitimate concern about some of these debates is the specter of demolishing the "good news" of the gospel of Jesus Christ. The strategy I will propose must address these legitimate concerns.

---

3. For books that present alternative views held by evangelicals on a variety of theological issues, see Boyd and Eddy, *Across the Spectrum*, and the various volumes published by Zondervan in their Counterpoints Series edited by Stanley N. Grundy.

Introduction

But there is another set of concerns coming from the other end of the evangelical spectrum, as pointed out by one of our contributors, Karl Giberson, whose perception is that Evangelicalism is moving to the "right" on both theological and political issues.

Giberson is particularly grieved by the significant number of evangelicals who are "patriarchal" and "anti-Muslim," who deny global warming, who express hostility to President Obama, who reject the idea of providing universal healthcare to all Americans, and who oppose any restrictions on guns. He is also concerned about the "hate" that is evident when such evangelicals express their views, concluding that "there can be no doubt that evangelicals cannot claim to be 'known by their love' as Jesus had hoped." Giberson's dismay is so great that he is now "uncomfortable with a label that carries as much negative baggage today as 'evangelical.'"

Although Giberson does not talk about policing boundaries in his posts, I gather that, for him, positions such as those stated above cross a boundary for acceptable evangelical belief and practice. The strategy I will propose must also address Giberson's legitimate concern.

EVANGELICAL BELIEFS AS A CENTERED-SET AND NOT A BOUNDED-SET

As prolegomena to my proposed strategy for productively navigating the diversity in evangelical belief and practice, I appeal to a distinction that has been made by Roger Olson. Drawing on set theory terminology in mathematics, Olson asserts that Evangelicalism can be viewed as "a centered-set category rather than as a set having boundaries," suggesting that in this view, "the question is not who is 'in' and who is 'out,' but who is nearer the center and who is moving away from it." Olson adds that "people gathered around the center or toward it are authentically evangelical; people or institutions moving away from it or with their backs turned against it are of questionable evangelical status."[4] Yet R.

---

4. Olson, *Reformed and Always Reforming*, 59–60. Olson lists this "centered-set" approach to theology as one of six "common features" that he

A Future for American Evangelicalism

Albert Mohler has a problem with Olson's distinction between a centered-set and bounded-set view of Evangelicalism, suggesting that "the moment the center is defined, boundaries necessarily appear."[5]

A possible way to navigate this disagreement is to note that Olson's position is dynamic, focusing on "movement" relative to a defined center. He notes that for the set-centered view, "the constructive task of theology is always open; there are no closed once for all systems of theology,"[6] adding the following reflection about the set-centered notion of "orthodoxy": "consistent and steady movement toward truth, guided by Scripture and tradition critically received, does make one orthodox."[7] In that light, it is possible to acknowledge "boundaries," but these boundaries are not fixed. Rather, they are defined in terms of proximity to the center and movement toward or away from the center. To be sure, such judgments are difficult to make; they will require conversations among evangelicals.

According to my reading of John Hawthorne's post, his perception of "young evangelicals" fits nicely with Olson's focus on the "center" of Evangelicalism: "younger evangelicals . . . aren't defining themselves by evaluating where the others are. They're looking for an authentic stance," which, I would add, can be provided by an appropriate "center."

Mark Sargent's take on the attitudes of recent students at the Christian colleges where he has served for many years fits well with Hawthorne's perception: "students are tired of jeremiads and are eager to know how to hold firmly to convictions and still participate in interfaith and pluralistic conversations that require prudent compromise and civil discourse to promote justice and

---

attributes to those evangelicals who embrace what he calls "the Postconservative Style of Evangelical Theology" (ibid., 53–65).

5. R. Albert Mohler Jr., "Confessional Evangelicalism," in Naselli and Hansen, *Four Views*, 76.

6. Olson, *Reformed and Always Reforming*, 55.

7. Ibid., 203.

Introduction

reduce violence." This nicely anticipates the strategy I will soon be proposing.

Of course, the thorny question remains as to what the "center" of Evangelicalism may be.

THE QUEST FOR COMMON GROUND AMONG DIVERSE EVANGELICALS

If evangelical belief can be viewed as a centered-set, then what is the "center?" My approach to answering this question is to seek to identify some common ground in the midst of the great diversity in evangelical belief and practice.

The most prominent attempt to identify such common ground among evangelicals comes from the British scholar David Bebbington. He has proposed that there are "four qualities that have been the special marks of Evangelical religion: conversionism, the belief that lives need to be changed; activism, the expression of the gospel in effort; biblicism, a particular regard for the Bible; and what may be called crucicentrism, a stress on the sacrifice of Christ on the cross."[8]

A number of our contributors appeal to Bebbington's list of characteristics, albeit with some paraphrasing, and in a few cases with some reservations. Corwin Smidt says that "such a listing . . . suggests that all evangelicals hold these four qualities," which "leaves unanswered whether those who subscribe to most, if not all, of the four specified beliefs are nevertheless considered to be evangelicals." Justin Barnard says that while "proposals that lean on Bebbington's quadrilateral" are "not without merit," they "seem strained by present sociological realities." Barnard goes on to cite the postings of Corwin Smidt, John Franke, and John Wilson to support this concern.

A prominent contemporary evangelical, R. Albert Mohler Jr., expresses concern about the "generality" of Bebbington's statement of characteristics: "David Bebbington's quadrilateral . . . points to

---

8. Bebbington, *Modern Britain*, 3.

the center of evangelical faith. But these cannot be left defined in terms as general as 'a particular regard for the Bible' and a 'stress on the sacrifice of Christ on the cross.' Left in these general terms, we know something of what an evangelical believes, but hardly enough to know then who is not an evangelical."[9]

What Mohler criticizes, I applaud. What he considers to be a weakness of Bebbington's quadrilateral, I consider a strength. It is precisely the "generality" of Bebbington's statement of characteristics that provides legitimate room for some differing interpretations that evangelicals need to talk about (as evidenced by the paraphrasing of some of these characteristics by some of our contributors). Therefore, I concur with Richard Mouw's assertion that "the four Bebbington marks of Evangelicalism . . . provide an excellent set of talking points." They are not the end of the conversation. They are only the beginning—a good place to start a conversation that needs to be sustained by evangelicals embedded in any given time and place.

Lest you think that the above paragraph reflects only my own point of view, I will illustrate what it says by going back to the postings of some of our contributors.

Amos Yong's posting is especially revealing. He concurs with Mouw in affirming that Bebbington's quadrilateral is "an adequate starting point." But Yong then elaborates on what may be called "a Pentecostal or renewalist twist on these Bebbington characteristics," adding that "such a twist . . . does not negate these central markers but is indicative of their evolving character."

For example, Yong asserts that "the substitutionary atonement of Christ's death remains central to renewal Christianity . . . [but] the cruciform work of Christ cannot be understood apart from the resurrecting power of the Spirit, and . . . the achievements of the person of Christ are intertwined with those of the Holy Spirit." Relative to "evangelical activism," Yong asserts that "Pentecostal missionary praxis may accentuate the workings of the charismata, in particular healings and miracles, underplayed by

---

9. R. Albert Mohler Jr., "Confessional Evangelicalism," in Naselli and Hansen, *Four Views*, 95.

Introduction

evangelical missiology." Yong also asserts that "evangelical conversionism understood along a Pentecostal register means not only a once-for-all turning away from sin but also the ongoing renewal and transformation in the path of Christ-following and Christian discipleship."

These assertions by Yong are not the final word. Rather, they are good starting points for conversation with those evangelicals who are not embedded in the pentecostal tradition.

Similarly, Corwin Smidt notes that affirmation of "biblical authority" (one possible paraphrasing of Bebbington's Biblicist assertion of "a particular regard for the Bible") has been viewed by some evangelicals as requiring a belief in "biblical inerrancy," while other evangelicals "subscribe to the older, and broader, notion of biblical infallibility." That difference should also be a starting point for further conversation.

Finally, Vincent Bacote regrets the fact that some evangelicals have interpreted Bebbington's biblicism in ways that marginalize the role of tradition. In his words, "one dimension of evangelical weakness stems from one of its strengths: fidelity to the Bible. Often the Reformation slogan *sola scriptura* is morphed into a view that places the Bible in an exclusive domain set apart from any notion of the larger Christian tradition." Obviously, more conversation is needed about the relationship between biblical authority and Christian tradition.

Believing, as I and a number of my contributors do, that Bebbington's quadrilateral is a good starting point for conversation—allowing for some differing interpretations of his general assertions—here is my personal paraphrase of his four characteristics, which I would love to talk about with other evangelicals. For each characteristic, I add relevant reflections from some of our contributors or additional comments that strike me as pertinent for ongoing conversations.

> *Biblicism:* The Bible is true in all that it affirms; it is an authoritative account of the Christian story of creation, fall, redemption, and consummation sufficient to inform Christian faith and practice; and its truths are to be

complemented by the truths about all of God's creation revealed by study in the various disciplines of knowledge.

The concept of "biblical inerrancy" does not mean that the Bible can be read as a science textbook. Phenomenological descriptions of the world contained in the Scriptures reflect the "location" of the ancient writers. For example, the three-tier universe described in Phil 2:6–11 is not meant to be a scientific description of the structure of the universe. Rather, the truth of this passage is that God emptied himself and revealed himself to us through a man in the person of Jesus.

Therefore, I believe the Bible is inerrant in the sense that it is true in all that it affirms, or all that it intends to say. This view of inerrancy does not assume that the Bible is self-interpreting. It points us to the necessary hermeneutical task of seeking the most adequate interpretation of biblical passages, taking into account the "location" of the authors, and considering the various genres in which they wrote.

The complementary relationship I propose between the truths revealed in the Bible and the truths revealed in the various disciplines of knowledge reflects my understanding of the "integration of faith and learning" ideal that is central to the stated missions of the Christian liberal arts colleges where I served for forty years. The cognitive aspect of such integration is the task of uncovering "integral connections" between the knowledge claims in the academic disciplines and biblical or theological understanding.[10] This search for connections is a two-way street. It seeks ways in which biblical or theological understanding illuminates knowledge in the academic disciplines. But it also seeks ways in which knowledge in the academic disciplines can illuminate biblical or theological understanding, which is the often-neglected second direction for this integrative quest. Given adequate interpretations in both of these spheres of knowledge, no contradictions will be uncovered, although we will never fully grasp all these connections.

---

10. Heie, "Christian Perspective," 95–116.

Introduction

> *Conversionism:* A Christian is a person who has made a commitment to be a follower of Jesus, aspiring to be conformed to the likeness of Jesus.

Vincent Bacote describes this characteristic as a "deep personal experience of conversion to Jesus." John Franke describes it as "a commitment to the importance of intentional discipleship in the way of Jesus." This does not mean that all Christians have to be able to point to a place or time when they had a dramatic "born-again" experience. But it does suggest that, whatever the means, every Christian has made a personal commitment to be a follower of Jesus. I believe that for those in the Reformed or Lutheran traditions, this means "growing into" the experience of grace bestowed by means of infant baptism. Those in "believers-baptism" traditions may wish to disagree.

> *Activism:* Christians are called to be agents for God's redemptive purposes, partnering with God in the task of reconciliation in all areas of life.

This characteristic zeroes in on what a number of our contributors noted as the central motif of the *evangel*, the good news of the gospel of Jesus Christ. Peter Enns points us to the importance of "the continuance of the gospel," while John Franke says that "as evangelicals we should continue to bear our distinctive and diverse witness to the truth of the gospel of Jesus Christ." Kyle Roberts refers to the "central passion for the gospel," with the important addendum that "by 'the gospel' I mean the story of Jesus of Nazareth, the son of God and risen Christ, who is reconciling sinners—and the created order—to God and who invites all believers to join in the project of reconciliation."

Note that Roberts embraces a broad view of the "project of reconciliation," in that all of God's created order "groans for redemption" (Rom 8:22). I also embrace this broad view of the good news of the gospel, based on the biblical teaching of Col 1:20 that through Jesus, "God was pleased to reconcile to himself all things, whether on earth or in heaven, by making peace through the blood of his cross."

A Future for American Evangelicalism

My current broad view of the good news of the gospel differs markedly from the narrower view I was exposed to in my Pietist Lutheran upbringing: that God only intends to save select individuals. It is clear that evangelicals disagree about the proper scope of the good news of the gospel, which calls for conversation.

Even when evangelicals agree on a broad view of the gospel, there are significant disagreements as to the best "means" to foster the redemption of all of creation. Some in the Anabaptist tradition see the world as so hopelessly broken that the only option for Christians is to model a "better way" in their Christian communities. Other evangelicals argue that it is only when people "get right with God" that they can redeem societal structures such as our broken political system. Others, like me, argue that there are "systemic evils" that need to be addressed by Christians but that do not necessitate prior conversions to the Christian faith. For example, the civil rights legislation in the 1960s would never have happened if we had waited until those who opposed such legislation "got saved." These disagreements beg for ongoing conversations among evangelicals.

> *Crucicentrism:* The reconciliation of all things to God is made possible by the life, death, and resurrection of Jesus Christ.

As noted by Bebbington in his original proposal in 1989, the means for reconciliation through Jesus Christ has typically been believed to be that of substitutionary atonement: "Belief that Christ died in our stead was not uniform in the Evangelical tradition, but it was normal."[11] However, there is currently disagreement among evangelicals regarding other possible theories of atonement, which call for much-needed conversation.

It is important to note the synergy between my articulations of these four characteristics of Evangelicalism around the integrative thread of "God's project of reconciliation": Crucicentrism holds that God's project of reconciliation, made possible through the life, death, and resurrection of Jesus Christ, extends to all areas

---

11. Bebbington, *Modern Britain*, 16.

Introduction

of life. Activism holds that Christians are called to partner with God in God's project of reconciliation. Conversionism points to the commitment to be a follower of Jesus that is to be the Christian's primary motivation for seeking to partner with God in God's project of reconciliation. And biblicism points us to the authority of the Bible as the primary source of teachings as how to understand our faith commitment and to put our profession of Christian faith into practice as we partner in God's project of reconciliation.[12]

In summary, I believe there is sufficient agreement among different streams of evangelicals about the four categories of Bebbington's quadrilateral, allowing for some differing interpretations and elaborations of each category to consider this quadrilateral as a "working center" for Evangelicalism that emphasizes "God's project of reconciliation." These differing interpretations of Bebbington's categories can then be the starting point for respectful conversations among evangelicals from the diverse streams of Evangelicalism.

Yet there are some significant obstacles that militate against evangelicals actually engaging one another in the type of respectful conversation that I hope for, a topic to which I now turn.

---

12. In his book *The End of Evangelicalism?*, David E. Fitch embraces a similar integrative thread, exhorting evangelicals to not compromise "the three central commitments so central to our history—a high view of Scripture, a conversionist soteriology, and a church active in society for its salvation" (his articulation of Bebbington's four characteristics, in which he combines activism and crucicentrism). But Fitch adds that Christians should reground these three commitments "in the triune work of God through Christ by the Spirit" in a way that will "shape evangelicals into a participation in his [God's] mission in the world" (ibid., 128). It is this regrounding that leads Fitch to reject the idea of the Bible being "inerrant according to the original autographs" in favor of understanding the Bible as "*our one and true story of God for the whole world—infallible in and through Jesus Christ our Lord,*" which bears similarities to my own articulation of biblicism.

A Future for American Evangelicalism

OBSTACLES TO RESPECTFUL CONVERSATION AMONG DIVERSE EVANGELICALS

I am not a sociologist, but some sociologist friends point to the apparent human need to maintain "group identity" by establishing clear boundaries between "us" and "them." To the extent that this is the case, some of those embedded in a given stream of Evangelicalism are not anxious to blur the boundaries between their own stream and other evangelical streams. This attitude clearly militates against engaging in respectful conversations across these various streams, since such conversation may lead to conversation partners having to rethink, and possibly refine some of their beliefs in light of the differing beliefs they encounter in each other.

This need to maintain strict boundaries between "us" and "them" is motivated by fear and is inimical to the genuine quest for Truth. It reflects a failure to put into practice a number of human virtues that evangelicals talk about as being "Christian virtues," as follows.

> *Humility:* The conviction that as a finite, fallible human being, I do not fully understand Truth as God knows it, and I can therefore learn from conversation with others, Christians, or non-Christians who disagree with me.

Such humility distinguishes between "Truth" and "truth," where Truth refers to the actual nature of things as God fully understands them, while truth refers to the partial glimpse that a finite, fallible human being can grasp of the Truth. At the same time that I believe there is Truth, I don't believe I typically have direct, unmediated access to that Truth. At best, I can aspire to grasp only a limited glimpse, for an aspect of the human condition is that "we see through a glass darkly" (1 Cor 13:12).

> *Patience:* The hope that through ongoing respectful conversations, greater understanding will gradually emerge as a gift.

Introduction

Chris K. Huebner beautifully captures the essence of such patience in his observations about the "nonviolent epistemology" of the late, distinguished Mennonite theologian John Howard Yoder. Huebner suggests that "theology operates according to a violent logic of speed whenever it is unwilling to risk the possibility that truthfulness is the outcome of ongoing, timeful, open conversation."[13] In contrast, "Yoder's nonviolent epistemology . . . assumes that truthfulness is an utterly contingent gift that can only be given and received and that it emerges at the site of vulnerable interchange with the other."[14] Therefore, Yoder "refuses to short-circuit debate and genuine engagement by moving on too quickly."[15] We must likewise overcome our own propensity to want quick answers to complex questions.

> *Love:* That enduring disposition of caring deeply for other people, which includes providing a welcoming space for them to freely express their points of view and engaging them in respectful conversation about our disagreements.

As 1 Cor 13:2 states, "If I have prophetic powers, and understand all mysteries and knowledge, and if I have all faith, so as to remove mountains, but do not have love, I am nothing." Jesus Christ has called all Christians to love others. My commitment to orchestrating respectful conversation with others is my deep-rooted response to that call.

A major obstacle to orchestrating the respectful conversations that are needed to get beyond evangelical divisiveness is that, despite our rhetoric, we evangelicals all too often fail to practice humility, patience, and love.

To those of us who have worked or are working at "evangelical institutions," there is another significant obstacle to having the type of respectful conversations that could ameliorate evangelical

---

13. Huebner "Scattered Body of Christ," 134–35.

14. Ibid. For further reflections on the nature of the "patience" that Yoder calls for, see Blum, "Yoder's Patience," 106–20, and Coles, "Wild Patience," 216–52.

15. Huebner, "Scattered Body of Christ," 136.

A Future for American Evangelicalism

divisiveness and help us to gain a better understanding of Truth as only God fully knows it: the pressure to avoid conversations that may upset the constituencies of these institutions, possibly to the point of withdrawing their support (a topic to which I will return later).

Peter Enns expresses this concern by asserting, "evangelical ecclesiastical and academic structures have a vested interest in maintaining a traditional evangelical model, and so do not easily tolerate calls for critical self-assessment and theological adjustment." He is especially concerned that the Fundamentalist stream of Evangelicalism that emerged in reaction to Protestant Liberalism and Modernism creates a mindset devoted to correcting other traditions, which inhibits embarking on "a journey of theological discovery."

In the face of such pressures at evangelical institutions, both evangelicals and our institutions need to embrace two additional virtues that I take to be "Christian virtues."

> *Individual courage:* Having the strength to freely give voice to one's convictions even when one's convictions may be unpopular.
>
> *Institutional courage*: The willingness to create safe spaces for those within the institution to freely disagree about important issues within the framework of agreed-upon core beliefs of the institution, even if that upsets the institution's supporting constituency.

Lest you think that my harping on the need for evangelicals to live out these Christian virtues is unrelated to the postings of our contributors, here are a few relevant contributor comments.

As John Hawthorne asserts, "evangelicals able to handle diversity in love speak to the best of the movement." Wyndy Corbin Reuschling wonders whether the "higher commitment to truth at all costs among evangelicals (at least in the form of propositional truth statements) as the supreme virtue" has come at "the expense of other important commitments, such as unity, love, kindness,

Introduction

compassion, forbearance, and a much-needed epistemic and personal humility."

Richard Mouw presents a good penultimate summary when, in reference to the "branding problem" that he believes evangelicals have these days, he asserts that "our 'branding' problem requires—in good part at least—a spiritual remedy. We need to cultivate a kinder and gentler Evangelicalism," adding that "my clear sense is that this is what the folks asking me what the 'evangelical' label should mean were hoping for. That very fact is for me a sign of hope for the future of the cause of the gospel!" Mouw astutely notes that those in the evangelical world in which he was raised (when talking about how Christians should behave in the "public arena") often quoted the first part of 1 Pet 3:15: "Always be prepared to give an answer to everyone who asks you to give the reason for the hope that you have." Yet "seldom . . . was the next part of the verse mentioned: 'But do this with gentleness and respect.'"

It is Jeannine Brown who describes most succinctly and eloquently the highlights of this chapter and the major contours of the strategy I am proposing for fostering respectful conversations among diverse evangelicals, phrased in terms of "the invitations that emerged" as she "engaged the posts" of our contributors on this first topic of our eCircle, adding an expression of appreciation for how "My colleagues [in this eCircle] have encouraged us toward an openness to difference, both within and outside of Evangelicalism." Brown writes of the eCircle as:

> An invitation to reflect on Evangelicalism as a movement with a history and a tradition of its own: By becoming aware of our locatedness, we might arrive at a potentially more modest self-assessment of our centrality within the Christian tradition that, paradoxically, could allow us to celebrate the diversity that is central to our identity.
>
> An invitation to recognize the breadth of our movement and face our inability to control the future trajectory of Evangelicalism, especially if that means forcing a single category or pattern upon the movement.

A Future for American Evangelicalism

> An invitation to offer, going forward, a more generous and kinder Evangelicalism that sees our growth tied, in part, to learning more from one another—across the diverse expressions of Evangelicalism that have been present throughout our history.

I am happy to accept Brown's invitations. It is my hope and prayer that many other evangelicals will join me in the respectful conversations that these invitations call for, which will be started in the chapters that follow.

2

Continuing the Conversation

In my introductory chapter, I concurred with proposals from Richard Mouw and Amos Yong that the four characteristics identified by David Bebbington as common ground among evangelicals were good talking points for beginning conversations about the diversity of evangelical beliefs.

I further applauded the fact that there is no one articulation of these four characteristics that evangelicals agree upon. This means that conversations starting with these talking points cannot help but begin with one or more articulations, the adequacy of which should be the first topic for conversation.

To get that conversation started, I then proposed my articulation of Bebbington's characteristics, as follows:

> *Biblicism:* The Bible is true in all that it affirms; it is an authoritative account of the Christian story of creation, fall, redemption, and consummation sufficient to inform Christian faith and practice; and its truths are to be complemented by the truths about all of God's creation revealed by study in the various disciplines of knowledge.
>
> *Conversionism:* A Christian is a person who has made a commitment to be a follower of Jesus, aspiring to be conformed to the likeness of Jesus.

A Future for American Evangelicalism

Activism: Christians are called to be agents for God's redemptive purposes, partnering with God in the task of reconciliation in all areas of life.

Crucicentrism: The reconciliation of all things to God is made possible by the life, death, and resurrection of Jesus Christ.

With that as background, here is my plan for the rest of this book: I will address, in turn, six major topics on which my contributors wrote after their postings on the introductory topic of "American Evangelicalism and the Broader Christian Tradition." Space does not allow me to present all their postings on these major topics. Rather, as I did in the introductory chapter, I will highlight those postings that I believe will serve best to "continue the conversation" about the subtopics (indicated by subheadings) I have chosen for each of the six major topics.

Although I am neither a theologian nor a biblical scholar, I will occasionally insert my personal reflections pertaining to a given subtopic in the hope of making a modest contribution to the ongoing conversation I envision, paying particular attention to the way in which the reflections of my contributors comport, or do not comport, with my particular articulation of Bebbington's proposed four components of common ground among evangelicals.

Of course, my selection of contributor postings to highlight and my personal reflections will be deeply informed by my purpose in writing this book, which is to present the contours of what I believe could be a vibrant future for American Evangelicalism if evangelicals can embrace the three demanding ideals of "commitment, openness, and conversation." Therefore, I take full responsibility for the contours that emerge in this book. I do not attribute any of them to my online contributors.

If someone else were to carefully analyze the 299 postings from my online contributors and the readers who submitted comments on their postings, he or she might come to a different set of conclusions that reflect his or her own particular interests and presuppositions. I certainly invite others to undertake that task for the purpose of initiating parallel conversations in their respective

Continuing the Conversation

spheres of influence, for I believe that the composite results of such conversations can help all evangelicals as we seek a better understanding of the nature of Truth as God fully understands it.

3

Evangelicalism and the Exclusivity of Christianity

THE EXCLUSIVE CLAIMS OF JESUS

Amos Young asserts most emphatically that "there is no doubt that Christian faith is exclusively in Jesus Christ," citing the very words of Jesus recorded in John 14:6: "No one comes to the Father except through me," and the proclamation of the apostles recorded in Acts 4:12: "There is salvation in no one else, for there is no other name under heaven given among mortals by which we must be saved."[1]

However, while granting that "for evangelical theologians, anyone who is 'saved' (united to God and redeemed from sin) is saved through and because of the life, death, and resurrection of Jesus," Kyle Roberts points out that the "question—and one that evangelical theologians are increasingly open to—is whether conscious awareness and knowledge of Jesus Christ and the Christian gospel is *necessary* to be positively and redemptively related to God."

---

1. NSRV.

Evangelicalism and the Exclusivity of Christianity

Roberts goes on to note that "exclusivists insist that explicit, conscious, and cognitive (even if minimal) knowledge of Jesus Christ is necessary for a person to be saved." But he then asserts:

> There are very few—if any—thoroughgoing exclusivists. Honest exclusivists recognize the challenges of the hard cases; this results in the granting of exceptions to the rule. What about the Old Testament saints—presumably none of whom knew about Jesus Christ in their lifetimes? What about the "man or woman on the island" who never had a chance to hear the gospel? What about infants who die? What about the mentally incapacitated—or victims of brain trauma? What about schizophrenics who can't tell the "voice" of Jesus from that of Satan? What about the victims of abuse who learned the "gospel" from their abusers? What gospel do they actually have? What Jesus—and what gospel—do they know?

Roberts concludes that "these hard cases suggest that 'accidental' features of history and situations outside one's choosing ought not to be *the* determining factor of one's eternal destiny." Based on these reflections on "accidental features of history," Robert's says that "perhaps . . . they suggest that the gospel cannot be reduced to propositional truths, to cognitive information," noting that "Jesus himself seemed to believe the gospel was not primarily about accepting cognitive propositions (Luke 4:18–19; Matt 25: 31–46; John 5: 31–40), but about God's grace of salvation, involving *relational* knowledge, resulting in transformed lives and societies."

So, Roberts asserts, the questions are: "How 'wide' is God's mercy? How accessible is God's grace? What kind of 'knowledge' is involved in salvation?" Roberts suggests that such knowledge has both a "cognitive, intellectual, and propositional" aspect and an "existential, relational, and experiential" aspect. This suggestion is similar to the view I expressed in my introductory chapter that a comprehensive understanding of what it means to be a whole Christian person calls into play the cognitive, affective, and volitional dimensions of personhood.

A Future for American Evangelicalism

Justin Barnard echoes Roberts when he asserts that "many evangelicals have regrettably reduced belief to mere cognition." Barnard suggests that this has "two unfortunate consequences":

> First, if salvation is primarily a function of explicit intellectual apprehension and self-conscious affirmation of the requisite set of propositions, this renders the prospect of redemption unlikely, if not impossible, for a whole range of persons for whom Christ died (e.g., very young children and the severely disabled). Second, an over-emphasis on procuring justification by belief-as-transaction tends to minimize the centrality of faithful obedience (John 14:15).

Barnard concludes that "perhaps, by grace through faith, one can begin to love God and follow Christ without yet fully understanding that it is Christ whom one is loving and following. Faith is, after all, God's gift."

John Franke adds another twist to the positions taken by Roberts and Barnard regarding the personal and relational nature of commitment to the Christian faith when he encourages us to rethink common ideas about the meaning of "truth." Franke writes, "This affirmation that Jesus is the truth is a stark challenge to the abstract ideas of truth we commonly hold," adding that "in Jesus we discover that truth is not merely intellectual or even moral, but personal and relational."

John Wilson and John Franke second the focus that emerges in Roberts and Barnard's postings on salvation as a gift from God that we should not presume to fully understand. Wilson writes, "How exactly Christ's redemptive work is accomplished in all times and places is not for us to say," while Franke adds that "the genuine significance of the church in the economy of God does not in any way imply that the church has been fully entrusted with authority or given control over the dispensation of grace in the world. These belong to God and God alone."

I personally resonate with the call from these four contributors to leave in God's hands the scope of God's extension of the gift of saving grace to those who do not have conscious awareness and

Evangelicalism and the Exclusivity of Christianity

knowledge of Jesus Christ and the Christian gospel. It is not for me to decide how gracious God wishes to be. I am content to witness to my own experience of God's grace (more about such "witness" later).

In summary, John Franke, drawing on the writings of Lesslie Newbiggin, provides a helpful, nuanced view pertaining to the ongoing debate about the exclusivist claims of Jesus Christ:

> He [Newbiggin] suggests that the Christian faith may be viewed as exclusive, inclusive and pluralist. It is *exclusive* in the sense of affirming the unique nature of the revelation of God in Jesus Christ, but not in the sense of denying the possibility of salvation to those outside of the Christian faith. It is *inclusive* in the sense of refusing to limit the saving grace of God to Christians, but not in the sense of viewing other religions as salvific. It is *pluralist* in the sense of acknowledging the gracious work of God in the lives of all human beings, but not in the sense of denying the unique and decisive nature of what God has done in Jesus Christ.

But it is John Wilson's grandmother who captures the essence of this section most simply with her response to John's questions about "all those people in China" and "those people who lived in parts of the world where there were no missionaries at all until recent times." In the words of John's grandmother, "God looks in the heart."

HOW, THEN, SHOULD WE EVANGELIZE?

If, indeed, God can work in marvelous, unexpected ways to extend the gift of grace to those who are not even aware of their experience of that grace, what are the implications for evangelism, the sharing of the good news of the gospel of Jesus Christ?

A number of our contributors have some strong views about how *not* to evangelize. John Hawthorne suggests that we need to avoid "posturing and a search for opportunities to find offense," focusing on the "separation between insiders and outsiders," and

A Future for American Evangelicalism

"thriving on being oppressed." Dan Russ warns us against "self-righteousness and condescension" and being "defensive." John Hawthorne and Jeannine Brown warn us against selling "salvation" as a commodity (as in the "I Found It" campaign). Kyle Roberts suggests that "to emphasize claims to exclusivity as a boundary marker clearly delineating the 'kingdom,' and then determining, on that basis, those who belong, is to miss the point of the gospel."

In sharp contrast, these contributors and others call for "extending welcome" (Jeannine Brown); "actual engagement" (John Hawthorne); and being "winsome" by "sharing the good news with grace and love" (Dan Russ).

But the resounding theme that emerges from posting after posting is that we should witness to the experience of grace in our own lives. This theme comports well with the incident reported in John 9 of Jesus restoring sight to a man who had been born blind. The Pharisees called into question this miraculous healing, trying to pressure the man to concede that Jesus was a sinner (v. 24). The man's profound response was: "I do not know whether he is a sinner. One thing I do know, that though I was blind, now I see" (v. 25). I am not competent to respond to all the thorny questions of those who question the Truth of the Christian faith. But I do know that I have experienced God's marvelous grace in my life, and I am happy to bear witness to that experience.

In a similar vein, Dan Russ observes that he has "found people very open to my 'witnessing' to them," elaborating that by "witnessing" he does not mean "attacking their beliefs, playing manipulative games with them, or forcing Christ down their throats." Rather, he means "what courts mean when the judge reminds the person being questioned by attorneys to stay with what they saw, heard, and experienced." Likewise, Jeannine Brown notes that "a witness points to truth or reality as they have seen it and experienced it," citing the way in which "the image of Jesus' followers as witnesses" is introduced in Luke 24: 46–48 and is "picked up in thematic ways in Acts."

John Franke further suggests that "the way of Jesus . . . is the way of humility and self-denial for the sake of others as a faithful

Evangelicalism and the Exclusivity of Christianity

witness to the love of God," while John Wilson says that "if the good news that Jesus proclaims is true, no apologies are necessary, no hesitation in sharing it is called for."

Kyle Roberts proposes that:

> evangelical Christians should let our conviction about Christ's centrality as the revelation of God motivate us to share, live, and witness to the message of God's reconciliation with humanity and promised redemption of the cosmos by extending Christ's presence in the world—by being the "peace" of Christ in a broken world . . . [W]e ought not be trying to convert people to evangelical Christianity. Rather, we ought to render witness by our lives, our love, our joy, and yes, by our words too, to Christ and the Spirit.

Note that Roberts has explicitly expanded the scope of our "witness" beyond testifying to our own experience of God's grace to include our witnessing to God's redemptive purposes for the entire cosmos. This reflects a significant broadening of the meaning of "evangelism" (witnessing to the good news of the gospel), a topic to which my contributors and I now turn.

A BROAD VIEW OF GOD'S REDEMPTIVE PURPOSES

Once again, John Wilson's grandmother most simply points us toward a broadened view of God's redemptive purposes. As Wilson describes, before going to China as a missionary around 1920 she "worked for a while as a city missionary in Aurora, Illinois. Much of the work she did there involved helping immigrant families. For her, providing practical aid was simply part of sharing the gospel."

Echoing Wilson's grandmother, Dan Russ asserts that many evangelicals today want to focus on providing such practical aid, in sharp contrast to a prevalent popular image of what it means to be an evangelical: "Many evangelicals today, tired of the right-wing, hateful, and often obnoxious image of our kind are simply trying to love our neighbors and our enemies, to take care of the homeless, the widows and orphans, and to care for the aliens among us without mentioning the reason we do so."

Amos Yong points us toward the same focus for our "Christian witness in a pluralistic world," writing:

> Apologetically . . . actions speak louder than words . . . Jesus and his followers touch hearts, heal bodies, and transform lives and communities. Christian mission in a pluralistic world is most effective when clear proclamation of the message of the gospel—of Jesus as savior, healer, sanctifier, and coming king—is preceded and supported by works of love, mercy, peace, and justice.

It is important to note that Wilson's grandmother, Russ, and Yong have all embraced a broad view of God's redemptive purposes. To be sure, God wishes to redeem individuals. But in addition to, not in place of, such individual redemption, God wishes to redeem all of the created order, and such broad redemption is made possible through Jesus Christ. This is clearly taught in Col 1:19–20: "For in him [Jesus] all the fullness of God was pleased to dwell, and through him God was pleased *to reconcile to himself all things*, whether on earth or in heaven, by making peace through the blood of his cross."[2]

My own Christian pilgrimage took me from a narrow to a broad view of God's redemptive purposes. Described in terms of Bebbington's concept of evangelical activism, the Pietist stream of Evangelicalism in which I was raised largely limited the good news of the gospel to the salvation of individuals. Primarily due to my immersion in the Reformed and Anabaptist streams of Evangelicalism, I now embrace a broad view of God's redemptive purposes that includes the redemption of all of creation, including the political realm[3] and other cultural and societal structures. It is for this reason that my articulations of Bebbington's activism and

---

2. Italics mine.

3. For my proposal as to how evangelicals can exert a redemptive influence in the political realm by orchestrating "respectful conversations" among those on both sides of the political aisle, see Heie, *Evangelicals on Public Policy Issues*.

Evangelicalism and the Exclusivity of Christianity

crucicentrism motifs emphasize that God's project of reconciliation encompasses "all areas of life."

Karl Giberson also wishes to point evangelicals toward a broad view of God's redemptive purposes. In his posting titled "The Hypocrisy of Christian Exclusiveness," Giberson is particularly critical of streams of Evangelicalism that focus on what he considers to be "theological hairsplitting" rather than on the challenges of loving our neighbors and the plight of the poor. Giberson writes:

> Somewhere along the way this theological hairsplitting became incredibly offensive to me. I no longer have any interest whatsoever in conversations about who has the right theology. It seems to me that these conversations are driven by some sort of jingoistic pathology—a defensive need to be a member of the one true tribe that holds "absolute truth" and maintains its hold on that truth by excluding others.
>
> I also think that this sectarian flag-planting has become a form of "easy Christianity," where the simple but significant challenges of Jesus to love our neighbors have been replaced with complicated but largely irrelevant discussions of who has the best handle on the "truth." This easy Christianity provides the consistent spectacle of fabulously wealthy white male religious leaders leading divisive and fractious movements on everything from gay marriage and contraception to the age of the earth and global warming while remaining absolutely silent on the plight of the world's poor. These are movements I am confident Jesus could not join, and leaders he could not follow.

While choosing to "take Karl [Giberson] as being a provocateur rather than as unkind," Ben Mitchell takes strong exception to his characterization of exclusivists as being "haughty and triumphalistic," citing the many splendid examples in church history of Christians enduring considerable hardship to share the good news of the gospel worldwide. Mitchell asserts that to label such Christians as "pathological jingoists" or hypocrites "would be a

31

terribly cynical and uncharitable reading of their lives," concluding with his perception that "some forms of inclusivism are even more authoritarian and mean-spirited than most exclusivist's claims."

HOSTS AND GUESTS IN CONVERSATION

Amos Yong eloquently describes the need for Christian witness to be embedded in the practice of being good "hosts and guests" in conversation with those committed to other faiths, religious or secular:

> I also think that given the goodness, truth, and beauty that is refracted through other cultural and religious traditions, Christians should be motivated to dialogue with those in other faiths not only missionally but also for our ongoing self-understanding. By dialogue, however, I don't mean only those formal occasions involving representative intellectuals but those circumstances when we can be hosts and guests of those in other faiths in order to get to know them, share our lives with them, and learn from them. The point of dialogue is that there is a mutuality of interaction, relationship, and transformation, just as when Peter met Cornelius (Acts 10). I mention being hosts *and* guests since sometimes, Christians are reluctant to embrace the latter role. It is simpler, and safer, to be hosts of those in other faiths since hosts establish the ground rules for the meeting. However, Jesus Christ himself is the paradigmatic guest himself in his incarnation even as the Holy Spirit desires to be the guest in every human heart. Christian missionaries have also been exemplary guests, as they are sent ones who enter into the spaces and times of others. Guests bring with them gifts—the gospel—but are also open to the hospitality of others, as Paul himself received such from the Maltese barbarians (Acts 28:1–10).

Note Yong's suggestion that our conversations with those committed to other faiths is not only for the purpose of our own

Evangelicalism and the Exclusivity of Christianity

witness, but also has the potential to contribute to our own "self-understanding." He elaborates:

> Do Christians really have anything to learn from others that they do not already know? . . . [T]here is no reason why authentic dialogical and conversational interaction with people of other faiths should not be catalytic for Christian self-transformation. Might not our interaction with religious others teach us humility, open us up to graces all humans hold in common, prompt questions about our own traditions (which are sometimes also encrusted in many ways by cultural accretions such that their original purposes have become obscured), and help us recognize that despite all we think we know, often in the face of reality we must be mute and wait for divine revelation to know how to "live, and move, and have our being"? Christian witness in a pluralistic world will surely bring about conversions to Christ, but it might also bring about Christian transformation, indeed revitalization and renewal.

Jeannine Brown echoes Yong's call for conversation in terms of "extending welcome," which combines both "witness and welcome." As Brown explains:

> I believe interreligious dialogue is essential in a world that is increasingly pluralistic. There is no upside to hiding in our churches and refusing to engage other faiths. Dialogue across faiths is essential for moving away from stereotyping and typecasting on either or both sides. Yet this is a minimalist (though initially important) reason for engaging in interreligious dialogue. Beyond this, we might engage people of other faiths in conversation for mutual understanding. They have something to offer us in terms of perspective on the good, the holy, and even the divine. We can affirm this truth, especially since we don't own Jesus. Rather, Jesus claims his ownership (Lordship) of us. And, yes, we engage people of other faiths in conversation with the hopes of introducing them to the Jesus we've come to know as Messiah and Lord . . . I am intrigued to imagine what it would it look

like for evangelicals to be gracious participants in interreligious dialogue . . . curious, not fearful, trusting in Christ and loving others well (1 John 4:18). What might it mean to hold as equally important the values of witness and welcome?

But Brown cautions us to avoid the temptation of Christians setting "ground rules for conversation" that reinforce power differentials. She warns, "we would do well to consider the power dynamics of conversations across difference, including those across religious lines. We can get at some of these power differentials by asking the questions, *Who's at the center and who's at the margins?* Or, *Who gets to set the parameters of the conversation?*"

However, Brown adds, some attitudinal ground rules may be appropriate:

> If by ground rules we mean that there are certain dispositions that will help interreligious dialogue begin and proceed effectively (especially because they attend to power differentials), then ground rules are apt. And I would commend the following dispositions for the conversation: respect, curiosity, conviction, and humility. Generally, we'll be better conversation partners if we've cultivated the competence of differentiation of self, by which we are able to share our own perspectives and convictions while paying attention to our anxieties that get hooked as we experience those who are quite different from us.

The call of Amos Yong and Jeannine Brown for evangelicals to "extend welcome" as good "hosts and guests" to those committed to other faiths gets to the heart of my purpose in writing this book: to call evangelicals to a form of engagement with others that embraces that rare and elusive combination of commitment, openness, and conversation.

4

Evangelicalism and the Modern Study of Scripture

THE AUTHORITY OF THE BIBLE

None of the contributors questions the "authority" of the Bible. For example, Peter Enns points to "the core commitment of the evangelical movement to the authority of Scripture." But such commitment does not answer the question posed by Rob Barrett: "In what sense is the Bible authoritative for American evangelicals?" Hopefully, the narrative that follows will respond adequately to that question.

ONE MODERN VIEW OF BIBLICAL INERRANCY

What does a Christian mean when he or she asserts that the Bible is "inerrant"? Molly Worthen suggests that the way "most American evangelicals now understand the term [inerrancy]" can be traced to Princeton Theological Seminary in the nineteenth century, the essence of which is captured by Charles Hodge's claim that "Scripture is a 'storehouse of facts.'" According to this view of inerrancy, to suggest the existence of "factual inaccuracies or discrepancies" in the Bible is to forsake belief in inerrancy.

But Worthen suggests that such a modern view of inerrancy may reflect "theological amnesia," since "the first generation of Reformers defended the authority of the Bible as a whole" and "were less inclined to haggle over Scriptures many apparent discrepancies." It appears that these early Reformers did not believe that if the Bible contains "factual inaccuracies or discrepancies," then it is "errant" and the authority of Scripture is compromised.

Worthen also reminds us we may be suffering from "theological amnesia" if we forget the diversity of "methods and assumptions" for "interpreting Scripture" across various streams of Evangelicalism that have not embraced a modern view of inerrancy:

> For centuries, evangelicals have drawn upon a wide range of methods and assumptions to interpret Scripture. Wesleyans have their "quadrilateral" of theological contemplation: church tradition, human reason, and personal experience should supplement Scripture in understanding God's will and cultivating a relationship with Christ. The Mennonites have long stressed the role of the community, the gathered saints, in discerning together the meaning of Scripture, and have worried more about discipleship than squabbling over "literal" interpretation. Pentecostals and charismatics read Scripture with the voice of God speaking audibly in their ears, telling them how to apply holy writ to their own lives.

According to one of our readers, Richard Pierard, the root problem relative to this modern view of inerrancy as requiring the absence of factual inaccuracies is that "it is a scientific, post-Enlightenment term applied to an ancient literary work."

The reflections of Worthen and Pierard suggest the need to think about the meaning of "inerrancy" in a new way, or rather the old way, once again.

Evangelicalism and the Modern Study of Scripture

ANOTHER MEANING FOR "INERRANCY"

There is another way to define "inerrancy" by which belief in inerrancy is not forsaken if we allow for the possibility of factual inaccuracies and discrepancies in the Bible.

Christopher Hays points us toward this alternative view of inerrancy when he says, "in popular discourse, we [evangelicals] tend to describe Scripture as authoritative, true, and without error. In broad strokes, I'm happy with that. But we all know there is a fair bit involved in figuring out *what Scripture is saying* in order to affirm that message as true." Justin Barnard echoes Hays when he asserts that "at its core, inerrancy is a commitment to the idea that the Bible is truthful in *all that it says*."[1]

I embrace this alternative definition of inerrancy because it doesn't bypass the challenging task of doing the biblical hermeneutics needed to ascertain exactly what it is that a particular biblical passage says, which may not require factual accuracy.

Ben Mitchell makes this way of viewing inerrancy more concrete with a particular example from Scripture:

> To say I believe the Bible is literally true does not mean that I believe that rivers have hands when the psalmist says 'Let the rivers clap their hands, let the mountains sing together for joy' (Ps 98:8 NIV). But I do believe that the salvation of the Lord makes his people jubilant! It just so happens, by inspiration of the Holy Spirit, that the author used the literary device of a psalm to communicate that *truth*."[2]

This example points to the importance of context and genre when interpreting the bible. Mitchell points to the "crippling" effect of not adequately taking into account context and genre when doing biblical hermeneutics: "One of the most crippling practices of evangelical culture is the flattening of the biblical text: *Sola Scriptura* was never meant to suggest that all Scripture was identical in

---

1. Italics mine.
2. Italics mine.

every way. The slogan does not justify ripping the biblical witness from its context or detaching it from its genre."

Jeannine Brown echoes Mitchell's concern about the "impoverishing" effects of neglecting "human context": "Neglect of the human context—the strange, lovely, and sometimes perplexing particularities—of the Bible by evangelical Christians is disturbing. And if inerrancy leads to a view of the text as a storehouse of facts and abstract principles to be extracted from the narrative contexts, then the reading it produces will be impoverished."

Brown also notes that granting a "human context" to Scriptures acknowledges that the Bible has a "human dimension" as well as a "divine dimension," which creates a tension that we need to navigate. Brown writes:

> There is a human and a divine dimension to the Bible. This means that faithful, proper interpretation of it will call for both human tools and for a reliance on God's illuminating presence. This explains, in part, why there will always be a tension or a challenging ambiguity when the Bible is read, and interpreted, and submitted to in the context of the church. If we want to avoid taming the text, we must embrace this tension and live together in it.

Christopher Hays suggests that "as a rule, we let ancient culture and literature modify our expectations of what the Bible is and how God uses it to reveal himself." For example, consideration of the level of knowledge, or lack thereof, of the nature of the cosmos on the part of the authors of ancient biblical texts, can reveal "factual inaccuracies" in the biblical narrative. An oft-quoted example is the way in which portions of Old Testament Scriptures describes the rising and setting of the sun: "The sun rises and goes down, and hurries to the place where it rises" (Eccl 1:5); or the sun "rises at one end of the heavens and makes its circuit to the other" (Ps 19:6). These descriptions reflect what Denis Lamoureux has called "an *ancient phenomenological perspective*. What the biblical writers saw with their eyes, they believed to be real, like the literal rising and setting of the sun." But their ancient understanding of

Evangelicalism and the Modern Study of Scripture

the cosmos is not "true." We now know that "the 'rising' or 'setting' of the sun is only a visual effect, caused by the rotation of the earth on its axis, giving us the appearance that the sun 'moves.'"[3]

These "factual inaccuracies" in no way detract from whatever truths these biblical passages are meant to convey. As in the example of Ps 98:8 pointed out by Ben Mitchell above, it is the task of biblical hermeneutics to uncover the truth of passages that transcend any such factual inaccuracies that reflect an outdated ancient cosmology.

As Andy Holt, a reader of this electronic conversation, asks, "Should an ancient document be judged by modern standards?" What Holt finds "unfathomably amazing [is] that whatever tiny errors of precision there may be (according to the standards of modern science) are absolutely inconsequential." But "inconsequential" compared to what? Inconsequential compared to the overarching purpose of the Bible, a topic to which the contributors and I now turn.

THE PURPOSE OF THE BIBLE

In a section of her post titled "Reading the Bible to Meet God," Jeannine Brown asserts that "the purpose of the Bible . . . is to reveal the living God to the people of God," adding that the Bible "facilitates the occasions for readers/hearers to listen to the voice of . . . God—and to respond." Brown goes on to say, "to not tame the text means to read, or hear, the Bible in anticipation of hearing the voice of God and meeting the Spirit of God."

Amos Yong adds an important dimension to Brown's assertion by suggesting that the Bible helps us to understand "God's intentions" for the world, which should inform our "praxis":

> The Bible is not just a set of propositions about past facts (although it certainly is that) but also a set of speech-acts where ongoing readings are performative modes of bringing about God's intentions (i.e., of saving the

---

3. Lamoureux, "No Historical Adam," 46.

world). In these senses, what Scripture meant and means cannot be divorced from what it was designed to achieve; reading and praxis, hence, are intertwined, as is meaning and application, to use more traditional notions.

Drawing on her own Wesleyan background, Wyndy Corbin Reuschling echoes Yong's assertion that praxis committed to "bring about God's purposes" is central to the purpose of the Bible:

> In my own Wesleyan context, Scripture's authority never rested in a particular idea about the Bible but in the Scripture's capacity to act as a means of grace connecting one with God, others, and with God's purposes in the world. Scripture's power and authority was in what it affects in the life of a believer. It is a functional authority, received by faith.

I resonate particularly with Corbin Reuschling's view of the Bible as "a means of grace connecting one with God, others, and with God's purposes in the world."[4] As readers will recall from the last chapter, I embrace a broad view of "God's purposes in the world" as encompassing the redemption of the entire created order, which has deeply informed my particular articulations of Bebbington's evangelical motifs of activism and crucicentrism.

Similarly to Molly Worthen's posting, Corbin Reuschling calls us back to the view of "biblical authority" that the Reformers embraced, saying, "Scripture is sufficient for salvation, Christian faith, practice, worship, devotion, and piety."

As Peter Enns pointed out, evangelicals do have a core commitment to the authority of Scripture. But it is a mistake to conflate biblical authority with a modern view of inerrancy that will not countenance any factual inaccuracies in Scripture. The concept of biblical authority must be understood in light of the purpose of Scripture, as elaborated in the above narrative.

These reflections have deeply informed my particular articulation of Bebbington's evangelical motif of biblicism. That is, the Bible is true in all that it affirms; it is an authoritative account of

---

4. See 2 Tim 3:16.

Evangelicalism and the Modern Study of Scripture

the Christian story of creation, fall, redemption, and consummation sufficient to inform Christian faith and practice; and its truths are to be complemented by the truths about all of God's creation revealed by study in the various disciplines of knowledge.

John Wilson states this motif more simply, quoting one of the "Covenant Affirmations" of the Evangelical Covenant Church, the particular stream of Evangelicalism where he has worshipped for many years: "We affirm the centrality of the Word of God." Wilson adds that in his decades of worship within this denomination, he "has not heard a single sermon on 'inerrancy,'" and I can say the same of my fourteen years of worship in the Evangelical Covenant Church.

By now, readers may surmise that I like the Evangelical Covenant Church's very general and minimalist affirmation of the evangelical motif of biblicism, since it creates space for disagreement, respectful conversation, and mutual learning as to the meaning of the words "the centrality of the Bible." My comparative verbosity as to the meaning of biblicism partially reflects my propensity to say in a lot of words what can be said in fewer words. But, more importantly, it reflects my desire to point to the integrative task of uncovering complimentary connections between the revelation of God in Scriptures and the ways God is revealed in those areas investigated by the various academic disciplines.

THE BIBLE FOR THE WHOLE CHRISTIAN PERSON

It is my perception that there is strong coherence between what the contributors have posted regarding the nature of the Bible, as reported in this chapter, and my contention in this book's introduction that a comprehensive understanding of what it means to be a "whole Christian person" encompasses the cognitive, affective, and volitional dimensions of personhood.

The Bible is intended to speak to all these dimensions of our personhood, not just to the intellect. Along these lines, Molly Worthen notes:

A Future for American Evangelicalism

The fundamentalist-modernist fights began in Reformed churches in the North, but soon spread throughout the country. Each tradition's fundamentalists had their own unique worries, but nearly all latched onto the slogan of biblical inerrancy. Denominational leaders like the Church of the Nazarene's Henry Orton Wiley watched with sadness as fellow believers abandoned their traditional approach to Scripture for Reformed fundamentalism. "Our danger is rationalism, which exalts the intellect to the detriment of the affections and the will," he wrote.

IS HISTORICAL CRITICISM PROBLEMATIC FOR EVANGELICAL THEOLOGY?

Whereas textual criticism of the Bible focuses on examining the text itself while disregarding or diminishing outside influences on the text, the emphasis in historical criticism (also called "the historical-critical method" or "higher criticism") is on the context in which the text was written, including consideration of the author's life, the history behind the biblical text, and the social circumstances at the time of writing. Thus the primary goal of historical criticism is to ascertain the text's original meaning in its original historical context.

Peter Enns sees "four general, interrelated, aspects of historical criticism that are well established in biblical scholarship and also, in various ways, at odds with mainstream Evangelicalism's understanding of the nature of Scripture." Since this subtopic is critical to the theme of this chapter, I will quote in full Enns' summary of the four interrelated aspects of historical criticism:

> 1. *Biblical origins.* The Old Testament we know today has a lengthy developmental history, both oral and written. The drawing together of these traditions did not commence in earnest until the Babylonian exile (sixth century BC) and did not come to an end until sometime during the Persian period (roughly fifth and fourth centuries BC) at the earliest. This does not mean that the Hebrew Bible was written out of whole cloth

Evangelicalism and the Modern Study of Scripture

during this period. Some books or portions of books clearly were, but many others were added to or updated in some way. Issues surrounding the formation of the New Testament are similar, but involve a much shorter period of time.

2. *Perspectives of the biblical writers.* When speaking of their past, the Old Testament writers were not working as modern historians or investigative journalists to uncover verifiable facts (as we might put it). They were more storytellers, conduits for generations—even centuries—of tradition, which they brought together to form their sacred text. In the Old Testament we have Israel's national-religious story as seen through the eyes of those responsible for giving it its final shape.

   This is not to say that they invented these traditions on the spot, but they "packaged" their past as they did to address their present crisis—exile, return, and an uncertain future. Israel's inscripturated story both accounts for this crisis and also points the way forward to the hope that God has not abandoned his people but has a glorious future in store for them.

   A similar issue holds for the New Testament, where the Gospels reflect the experiences and thinking of various Christian communities a generation and more after Jesus' ministry on earth. They, too, are presentations of Jesus and the early missionary activities that reflect the perspectives and needs of the respective communities.

3. *Theological diversity.* Given historical criticism's focus on matters of biblical origin, the diversity of the various biblical texts is highlighted with no pressing concern, as we see in Evangelicalism, to draw these diverse texts into a harmonious whole. Hence, historical criticism speaks freely of the different *theologies* contained in Scripture.

   One practical implication is that the evangelical hermeneutical methodology of allowing "Scripture to interpret Scripture" tends to fall on deaf ears among historical critics. Reading Genesis, for example, through the eyes of Isaiah or Paul *in order to understand the meaning of Genesis* would be like reading Shakespeare through the eyes of Arthur Miller and expecting to gain from it an insight into what Shakespeare meant.

4. *The problem of historicity.* This last aspect of historical criticism in effect summarizes the previous three: the Bible does not tell us what happened so much as what the biblical writers either believed happened or what they invented. This is not to say that historical critics think nothing of historical importance can be found in Scripture, but that any historical information is inextricably bound up with the perspectives and purposes of the biblical writers.

A sticking point for many evangelicals regarding the method of historical criticism, as summarized above, is the "human dimension" that is attributed to the Bible. Such evangelicals believe that the authority of biblical revelation is somehow diminished when we allow for such a human dimension. Karl Giberson goes so far as to assert that "very few evangelicals ascribe *any* meaningful human dimension to Scripture." A number of our evangelical contributors strongly acknowledge such a human dimension.

As already noted in our discussion of the importance of considering context when interpreting Scripture, Jeannine Brown asserts:

> There is a human and a divine dimension to the Bible. This means that faithful, proper interpretation of it will call for both human tools and for a reliance on God's illuminating presence. This explains, in part, why there will always be a tension or a challenging ambiguity when the Bible is read, and interpreted, and submitted to in the context of the church. If we want to avoid taming the text, we must embrace this tension and live together in it.

Amos Yong echoes Brown when he says, "there is a growing realization that a presupposition-less exegesis is well-nigh impossible."

Evangelicalism and the Modern Study of Scripture

One of our readers, posting under the name "Christian Vagabond," puts it more colorfully: "It [the Bible] reflects divine truths about God without revealing the full truth or freeing itself of its human origins. In short, I believe that the Bible is divinely inspired, but it's a divinely inspired mess, and that's what God intended it to be."

My own way of making sense of both the divine and human authorship of the Bible is to say that the "truths" we discern from the biblical record are mediated through the words chosen by human authors, which inevitably reflect their social locations.

Peter Enns suggests that these disagreements among evangelicals as to the validity of historical criticism will not be sorted through any time soon: "The tensions between evangelicals and historical criticism have not been settled, nor will they be in the near future, at least as I see it," adding that "there seems to be an implicit détente."

But Enns hopes for more that détente. He hopes for an eventual "explicit synthesis between evangelical theology and historical criticism in order to achieve, potentially, a more lasting peace." However, the "difficulty," as Enns sees it, "is that such a synthesis might threaten the very structure of Evangelicalism to the breaking point." Is such a synthesis possible? I, and some of my contributors, embrace that possibility, assuming that evangelicals can learn to talk to one another about this contentious issue. I need to elaborate.

AN OPPORTUNITY BEGGING FOR CONVERSATION

One of our readers, Phillip Cary, agrees with Peter Enns that there is presently détente relative to historical criticism. But Cary asserts that "the détente is not a bad thing, . . . it is temporary," adding that a position being temporary is a characteristic of "every position we take in a conversation where we're learning things." Therefore, Cary concludes that "the détente is nothing to be ashamed of but also nothing to put a great deal of trust in. We've got to keep learning."

Cary also notes that having ongoing conversations about contentious issues is normal for any "healthy intellectual tradition," in contrast to a tradition that has become "moribund." Referring to the conversation that is taking place in this eCircle on American Evangelicalism, Cary asserts that:

> the kind of conversation we're involved in, right now, is the ordinary kind of thing that happens in any intellectual tradition. As Alasdair MacIntyre points out, an intellectual tradition is largely constituted as an ongoing argument about what belongs to the tradition. That argument about itself is part of its health. It's only when you stop arguing and asking questions that the tradition becomes moribund. So one of the things we should do is resist the kind of anxiety that would lead us to try to shut down the conversation, suppress questions, etc.

Cary also affirms Enn's observation that "each new generation of evangelical scholars questions where the lines have been drawn and rejects some of the older solutions," adding that this "also means that we don't know in advance where the conversation will lead us" (which I quote with delight since one of the lynchpins of my work these days is my belief that "you cannot predict beforehand the results of a respectful conversation").[5]

Recalling Peter Enn's concern that an attempt to synthesize evangelical theology with historical criticism "might threaten the very structure of Evangelicalism to the breaking point," Christopher Hays builds on Phillip Cary's assertions by suggesting that our only option is to encourage our "best and brightest" evangelical scholars to attempt this synthesis (without attempting to predict beforehand the results of the conversations that will be part of such an attempt at synthesis):

> I'm not saying that we should do historical criticism just so that the cool kids at SBL will let us sit at their tables.

---

5. Harold Heie, "Mission," *Respectful Conversation*, 2013 http://www.respectfulconversation.net/mission.

Evangelicalism and the Modern Study of Scripture

(They already do!) I am saying that historical criticism raises questions that demand more attention than we've hitherto given. It *may* be that historical criticism will prove a bull in our dogmatic china-shop, that we've got to lock it out because it cannot but shatter our theology. But we don't *know* that to be the case yet, because our best and brightest have not engaged historical criticism with the same vigor that they've applied to exegesis, linguistics, and doctrine.

Amos Yong observes that willingness to engage those who disagree with us about difficult issues—such as an attempted synthesis of evangelical theology with historical criticism—presupposes openness to "self-correction." He asserts that "readers are edified when they understand the biblical text in its original context," adding:

> For me, the motivation of the critical approach is the key. If not from the standpoint of faith, then criticism persists for its own sake. On the other hand, believers ought to, in faith, pursue questions as they might appear. Truth is truth, wherever it may be found, and scholars and researchers ought to pursue such within their various communities of inquiry. Many such matters will be contested, and it is part of the life of faith, and of the scholarly vocation, to engage with these issues. Will there be casualties? Yes! Can these be minimized if evangelical scholarship is nurtured in part within faithful communities of inquiry? Absolutely. The end result is a more robust, world-engaging, insightful, and fruitful Christianity that probes deeply, analyzes critically, self-corrects over time, and increases community understanding and spiritual growth.

John Hawthorne echoes Amos Yong in his reflection on Yong's posting calling for a new mode of engagement with those who disagree with us: "As Amos Yong observes, maybe attentiveness to the Spirit can lead to a new rhetorical style, one that seeks to engage the other rather than winning the argument."

A Future for American Evangelicalism

OBSTACLES TO CONVERSATION ABOUT HISTORICAL CRITICISM (AND OTHER CONTENTIOUS ISSUES)

Our contributors and readers point to a number of obstacles to engaging in fruitful conversations about historical criticism and other issues that give rise to strong disagreements concerning biblical interpretation. One reader, Dan Knauss, notes a few obstacles to the "serious self-questioning" that is necessary if such conversations are to be authentic: "Within the community of the elect conflict-aversion and a pretence of unity becomes habitual, stifling curiosity, creativity and serious self-questioning."

Jeannine Brown points to a common tendency for evangelicals who hold to the modern view of inerrancy that a number of our contributors and I have called into question above to "exchange the authority of God for our own authority. What becomes authoritative, then, are our inherited, cherished *interpretations* of the Bible." This suggests a need for us to be open to the possibility that some of our "cherished interpretations" may be inadequate, which presupposes a significant measure of humility.

John Hawthorne warns us against the danger of "conversation-enders," even suggesting that the ways we use Scripture can abruptly end a conversation: "many evangelicals use Scripture as a rhetorical weapon. In short, Scripture is too often used as a conversation-ender and not a means of hearing God speak to all listeners."

My own approach to addressing Hawthorne's concern is to start any conversation with a search for common ground relative to the content of the various positions that are expressed, without abruptly ending the conversation by prematurely appealing to the "sources" of the various positions being taken.[6] Recall also my claim in the introduction to this book that, in addition to the attribute of humility that Jeannine Brown points us toward above, for conversations with those who disagree with us to bear fruit, we also need to exemplify the attributes of patience, love, and courage.

---

6. Heie, "Dialogic Discourse," 347–56.

Evangelicalism and the Modern Study of Scripture

A CAUTION FOR AMERICAN EVANGELICALS

It is fitting to conclude this chapter with the reflections of Nina Balmaceda, which bring us back to the significant role of social location and context in our various interpretations of the Bible and leads to some serious implications as we orchestrate conversations with others about contentious issues:

> We must not ignore that all readers will also bring their own cultural lenses to the interpretation of the biblical text. So, those who seek understanding of the things of God through the Scriptures need to be aware of the limitations imposed by that fact, realizing that since we are living in a different location and culture, we may be missing some important aspects of the message in interpreting the biblical text.

Balmaceda goes on to caution us that some evangelicals in America may be interpreting portions of the Bible in the "comfortable" and "individually" oriented culture of America, which makes them oblivious to certain biblical themes that jump out at Christians living in dire circumstances. Balmaceda writes:

> As an observer of different groups of evangelicals in the United States, I think that many believers do not realize how much contextualization they apply in their interpretation of the Bible. It should be noted that the relevant question here is not whether we should contextualize the Scriptures (we all do it), but whether we are able to contextualize it well enough. Many middleclass evangelical believers I have met in the United States approach the Scriptures from the context of a relatively comfortable life experience and a predominantly individualistic cultural mindset. The message of the gospel tends to be reduced, through contextualization, to an understanding of God's relation to human beings in individual, and rather isolated, ways. Christianity tends to be interpreted by many as God relating to the individual separated from his or her community.
>
> As a result, the references to certain biblical themes such as the promise of liberation, the quest for justice,

and the need to end or minimize oppression, among other relevant ones, are simply reduced to purely spiritual or mystical expectations. Understanding the Bible in this way diminishes the profound meaning of the Bible in all areas of life and our understanding of what God's demands of Christians in a very unjust world.

A powerful implication of these reflections on the differing contexts that inform different interpretations of the Bible for the conversations we orchestrate is that we need to include as conversation partners those whose social locations differ from ours, listening carefully to what they have to say since they may have important insights into the meanings of certain biblical passages that elude us because of our particular context. To quote Balmaceda again,

> The ethical values that are inherent to the kingdom of God that Jesus introduced in this world can be better understood when we are willing to hear what the message means to those who suffer oppression and/or marginalization. Listening to biblical interpretations from more community-oriented believers can help us discover the depth of the message of the gospel beyond the terms of an individual relationship with God. The kingdom of God is not only a future reality, or a reality in a different cosmic dimension, the kingdom has come in the person of Jesus Christ and he inaugurated a new era for human beings, bringing down the barriers of separation that human beings tend to build. In the American context, believers need to be aware of the barriers that excessive individualism can build . . . We must always remember that our understanding of God's Word is heavily influenced by our own cultural lenses and life experience through which we read it. This is why we need to remind ourselves to listen to each other as we approach the Scriptures.

5

Evangelicalism and Morality

I anticipated that a number of our contributors would address some specific hot-button moral issues of our day, such as same-sex marriage, abortion, healthcare, or gun control. With one exception, that did not emerge.[1] The one exception was the posting by Ben Mitchell titled, "Evangelical and Human Dignity." Mitchell said that "preserving a robust notion of human dignity seems to me to be a task worthy of evangelicals in the twenty-first century."

Mitchell asserts, "our humanity begins *in utero*. We are human beings from conception." He observes that "the Hebrew doctrine of the 'sanctity of human life' provided the moral framework for early Christian condemnation of abortion and infanticide," adding that "Christians did not merely condemn abortion and infanticide, however, they provided alternatives, adopting children who were destined to be abandoned." Mitchell's summary conclusion is that "the witness of Scripture and the testimony of the early church is that every human being, from conception through natural death is

1. For a narrative that addresses some contemporary contentious moral issues see Heie, *Evangelicals on Public Policy Issues*, in which six evangelicals with diverse political views take positions on the following public policy issues: the federal budget deficit, immigration, religious freedom, Syria and Iran, Israel and Palestine, poverty in the United States, marriage, healthcare, K-12 education, gun control, abortion, and the role of government.

to be respected as an imager of God whose life has special dignity in virtue of his or her relationship to the Creator. The doctrine of human dignity is written into the warp and woof of biblical faith."

The postings of other contributors focused on issues often identified as "meta-ethical" (about ethics), as follows.

SOCIAL JUSTICE

Christopher Hays notes, "Social Justice still polarizes Evangelicalism." Hays and other contributors point to two reasons for such polarization. The first is the question of who should be the agents for fostering social justice.

Relative to the issue of addressing the needs of the poor, those evangelicals who situate themselves toward the "right" end of the political spectrum are "affirming the place of charitable giving to the poor and to para-church organizations," while "the evangelical left tends to be much more optimistic about the efficacy of government interventions," as Hays writes.

Another aspect of the polarization among evangelicals about who should address social justice issues is the many differing views about the business sector. As Hays explains, "if 'Big Government' is the *bête noire* of the right, 'Big Corporations' are the villains of the evangelical left." For example, many on the right tend to see the business sector as the solution to the problem of poverty (e.g., by providing the jobs needed by the poor). Many on the left tend to see the business sector as the cause of the problem of poverty (e.g., by underpaying employees to maximize profits).

Before proceeding, it is important to note that these two reasons for polarization among evangelicals about how best to meet the needs of the poor is a disagreement as to "means," not "ends." Most Christians at both ends of the political spectrum agree that Christians should address the needs of the poor. What they primarily disagree about is the best "means" toward accomplishing that worthy "end."

A second reason for polarization among evangelicals is disagreement as to the relationship between "individual morality"

Evangelicalism and Morality

and "social morality." Those who, as John Hawthorne writes, hold to the "primacy of individual morality over social morality" tend to diminish the importance of talking "about broad issues like inequality, racism, the environment, immigration, [or] the common good," which are all "moral questions."

In a similar vein, Wyndy Corbin Reuschling attributes a "divide between personal and social ethics" to "the influence of individualism in American culture." She explains:

> This emphasis on the individual as both the target and source of change (i.e., "saved" people will "save" society) contributes to a constructed divide between personal and social ethics. This impacts how evangelicals tend to use Scripture in ethics and analyze social issues, which are often viewed merely as the extension of personal problems or individual moral failures, ignoring the systemic, contextual, and historical roots of many social ethical issues.

Those evangelicals who focus on social justice reject the view that social ills are merely extensions of personal problems or individual moral failures. Rather, there are systemic ills that must be addressed directly, instead of waiting for individuals to be "saved" so that they can then address such social ills.

IS BALANCE RATHER THAN POLAR OPPOSITION CALLED FOR?

I am struck by how the polarization described above buys into either-or thinking that rejects the possibility of the both-and solutions that reflect appropriate balances. Why do we posit inevitable opposition between private and ecclesial efforts versus the efforts of government in assisting the poor? Can't it be both? Is the problem of poverty so great that it has to be both? Why do we posit opposition between "individual morality" and "social morality"? Doesn't the Bible teach that Christians should be concerned about both?

Two of our contributors note the need for both-and approaches. Christopher Hays asserts that "the Christian pursuit of justice and mercy will likely be best served if our ecclesial and private generosity is coupled with the pursuit of progress through both government *and* business." Likewise, Amos Yong asserts that "on moral issues, we ought not to be fixated on one of these (like homosexuality) to the neglect of others related to the breath of the lifespan. Beginning and end of life issues are no more or less important than war, immigration, poverty, medical accessibility, and disability."

Life is relatively simple if we fixate on one pole of an either-or dichotomy. Things get more complicated if we embrace a both-and approach, since this approach raises the need for discernment as to the proper balance between both poles[2] (e.g., What is the appropriate balance between private and ecclesial generosity and governmental efforts in addressing the pressing needs of the poor?). Striking such a balance on any given moral issue requires that those deeply committed to the efficacy of one pole talk respectfully to those equally committed to the efficacy of the other pole so that, together, they can see whether common ground can be reached as to the most efficacious balance.

CONVERSATION AS A STRATEGY TO SEEK BALANCE

Conversations between two people holding to polar opposite viewpoints will get nowhere if either party sees absolutely no value in the position of the other. Therefore, as pointed out by Christopher Hays, each party needs to "learn to value" the "other's point of view." Touching again on the possibility that many evangelicals might agree on the "end" of social justice but disagree strongly on the best "means" for fostering social justice, Hays asserts that "very few evangelicals today will write off the place of social justice among Christian moral concerns. Nonetheless, we will make more

---

2. I discuss this need for balance in addressing public policy issues in Heie, *Evangelicals on Public Policy Issues*, 139–42.

Evangelicalism and Morality

moral progress in the practices of justice and mercy if those on the evangelical right and left learn to *value each other's point of view.*"

But how does one get from seeing absolutely no value in the other's point of view to learning to value that point of view? This huge gap is best navigated by the two parties getting to know one another sufficiently to gain mutual understanding as to the reasons for the other person's position, which can be deeply informed by elements of the other person's individualism, such as ethnicity, gender, socioeconomic status, being embedded in a particular religious tradition (like a particular stream of Evangelicalism), or personal biography.[3]

Kyle Roberts expands, possibly provocatively, on how various elements of our particularities inform our moral points of view, including the "developmental process of socialization" and even our biological makeup:

> The interesting question is, and one that cognitive psychology is increasingly pressing upon is, *how much does conscious choice and rational reflection play into our moral preferences?* The answer they give: *far less than we think.* Much of our moral preferences and behavior are responses of intuitions and affective preferences, many of which were lodged into our brains long before we learned to speak. We enter human existence with a pre-formed moral architecture, which is mollified, shaped, and confirmed or challenged through the process of human development and socialization.
>
> If morality is at least, in some sense, a product of evolution (or if its building blocks are) and if our moral responses comprise a combination of internal, emotive reactions and a developmental process of socialization, then this raises a number of interesting questions about "biblical morality." Not only might we be quicker to reflect on our own moral preferences and impulses, but we might also slow down and think about how our biology and our social context impacts our interpretations of the Bible. I've seen a number of blog posts recently on the phenomenon of "cherry picking" the Bible to support

3. Monsma, "Salt and Light," 21–36.

our preformed moral preferences. We all cherry pick to some degree, but the more we are aware of the various factors undergirding and motivating our cherry picking, the greater will be our capacity to responsibly reflect on our biblical interpretations and moral conclusions.

Roberts suggests that it may be because of our differing paths of socialization (and even our differing biological makeups) that "we find Christians who emphasize holiness, purity, and separation, and Christians who prefer compassion, nurture, and inclusion. We have Christians who gravitate toward authority and hierarchy, and Christians who lean toward equality and democracy."

If our positions on moral issues are deeply informed by our individual particularities, this raises the specter of "relativism"— your position is based on who you are and where you have been, and the same is true for me, so there is no way to reconcile our disagreements.

That is not the case if we are willing to be exposed to "alternative biblical interpretations and moral perspectives" and then talk about our disagreements. As Roberts puts it:

> Perhaps the best antidote to an unreflective, entirely intuitive moral structure is intentional exposure to alternate biblical interpretations and moral perspectives. As a white, male, American Christian, I ought to read and listen to perspectives on Scripture and morality from Christians and others who occupy contextually different perspectives on morality. This intentional exposure doesn't force me to change my perspective, nor does it require epistemic or moral relativism; it does, however, remind me of the possibility that I might not be in possession of the absolute truth. I might not have the correct "biblical" interpretation, and I *certainly* don't have the only or final word on a complex, moral issue.

Note the importance attributed by Roberts to "reading and listening to perspectives on Scripture and morality of others who occupy contextually different perspectives on morality," especially those who are not white, male, American Christians.

Evangelicalism and Morality

Vincent Bacote strikes a similar chord when he asks, "Who gets to frame the ethical conversation?" Bacote adds that the conversation needs to include those "whose voices are either muted or ignored," asking,

> Who gets to frame the ethical conversation? Who gets to say what counts and what gets "airplay"? I ask this not to swing the pendulum in one direction and completely change the conversation, but to expand the conversation and to challenge us to consider what ethical challenges face those whose voices are either muted or ignored. In some cases, this means considering how "perennial" issues have dimensions that are magnified in the lives of those off our radar, and in other cases, it means surveying the metaphorical ethical landscape to see if those on the margins are asking ethical questions that we have ignored or haven't recognized. Perhaps we can frame the question this way: How do we do a better job of recognizing the ethical concerns in front of us, especially when the ethical questions are raised by those who are not in power or those who tend to be invisible to us? There is a great opportunity here for evangelicals to lead the way, but we have to recognize the ways we are myopic in vision and captive to tendencies that enable us to disregard those on the margins.

Ted Williams and one of our readers, Rein Vanderhill, both have strong words of caution for those who think that the conversation ought to be dominated by American Christians. Reminding us that George Washington "called religion and morality 'indispensable supports' of 'political prosperity,'" Williams asserts:

> Unless we acknowledge the distinctive role that the faith community can play in promoting values like sacrifice, peace, delayed gratification, humility, and responsibility to family and community, America's demise will be similar [to that of the Roman Empire]. Changing the political discourse to respect the historic position of religion in free societies, and understanding its unique place in solving our current dilemmas, is America's only way forward.

A Future for American Evangelicalism

This dim view of the extent to which American culture now embraces the values needed for "political prosperity" suggests that ethical conversations dominated by American voices, as they are presently constituted, will be severely distorted.

Vanderhill expresses an even stronger concern about embarking on conversations that are dominated by "American voices," suggesting that these "political values" will be difficult to inculcate in American society, which is now characterized by "extreme economic disparity":

> Values such as peace, delayed gratification, humility, and responsibility to family cannot be inculcated at any large scale within a society of extreme economic disparity . . . By focusing on the poor as morally deficient, the evangelicals present to them an almost impossible goal and at the same time hand an excuse to that small fraction of those in our country whose moral failure is that of greed.

Another word of caution is expressed by Christopher Hays in his response to the posting from Karl Giberson:

> Karl, I think you are right that social justice has got to be the most significant moral issue addressed in the Scripture (maybe idolatry outstrips it?), and the way it's been overlooked in recent history (and continues to be overlooked today) certainly does speak to the degree to which our Christianity has been syncretized with a particular set of politico-economic ideologies.

The conversation I call for, as a strategy for seeking balance between opposing views on how best to foster social justice, will be impossible if those on either side of the political aisle will not budge from "politico-economic ideologies," which will be discussed further in the next chapter.

A conversation among evangelicals about seeking balance between opposing views on how to foster social justice must certainly be informed by our understanding of what the Bible teaches about morality, the second major meta-ethical issue that emerged in our eCircle and a topic to which I now turn.

Evangelicalism and Morality

THE ROLE OF SCRIPTURE REGARDING MORAL ISSUES

In commenting on the role of Scripture for informing decisions about moral issues, John Hawthorne asserts, "The Scriptures provide us with guidance of general principles . . . but not specific answers. They suggest the answer is 'somewhere in that general direction' without drawing the line in the sand," adding his view that "simple answers that sell books in Christian bookstores" will not suffice in our complex world.

Vincent Bacote describes the challenge of applying general moral principles found in Scripture to specific contemporary moral issues in the following way: "How one traces the trajectory from divine revelation to ethical decision making . . . is a challenging task because of a range of questions, including those related to bridging contexts and determining not only the proper interpretation of texts, but also the relevance of texts to our contemporary setting." Rob Barrett echoes the challenging nature of this task when he frames the conversation on "Evangelicalism and Morality" with the assertion that "the line between applying Christian morality to new situations and compromising our morals can be quite difficult to discern."

In one of the "leading questions" that Barrett poses for our contributors, he complicates matters further by observing that there have been "past changes in Christian moral norms (for example, on slavery or birth control)"—precipitated, I would add, by refined interpretations of Scripture—that "inform engagement with pressures to re-work Christian perspectives on today's hot issues (for example, homosexuality or social justice)."

Still further complication arises in Wyndy Corbin Reuschling's response to another one of Rob Barrett's leading questions: "To what degree is moral formation a cognitive activity of working out what is right or wrong, versus a *character activity* of building habits of moral actions?"[4] Corbin Reuschling responds as follows:

---

4. Italics mine.

A Future for American Evangelicalism

While evangelicals may claim that the Bible is authoritative in ethics, how Scripture's authority actually applies to making moral judgments is another matter. My hunch is that most evangelicals view the Bible as a rule book or moral manual of sorts for making ethical decisions. The hermeneutical difficulties of this approach should be obvious. Not only is this approach to Scripture's role in ethics reductionistic, it also reflects an understanding that ethics is simply making decisions or following rules . . . But this is not the task of ethics . . . Ethical reflection, responsibility and response start with us, with who we understand ourselves to be in light of God's call and purposes, what we ought to be about and care about, and how we ought to live. Moral formation is about learning to live more coherently, with integrity if you will, between what we profess to be true and living truthfully in all areas of life. This is a much harder task than the lobbying for various moralisms, for it requires an ongoing, honest self-examination of our lives over the course of our lifetime in open conversation with Scripture, Christian community, and with eyes wide open to the realities of our world. Christian moral formation and growing in our ethical sensibilities are concerned with who we are, how we live, and what we *actually* do. I suggest, therefore, that moral formation and the development of character (should) go together given the learned, practiced, and concrete dimensions of both. Equal attention and importance must be given to who we are, what we believe about what is "good, true, noble, and just," *and* how we act.

If Corbin Reuschling is correct that living ethically is not just about what we believe to be "true, good, noble, and just," but is just as much about the development of "character" in ways that empower us to "act" on what we say we believe, this has implications for what we hope to gain by the reading of Scriptures. In my estimation, it allows for reading the Bible for instruction relative to character formation, and even as "a source for growth in personal piety." But as Corbin Reuschling points out, to limit our reading of the Bible to that one dimension related to character development may be truncated: "We may read the Bible simply as a source for

Evangelicalism and Morality

growth in personal piety while ignoring the very social dimensions and contexts of Scripture, and the moral issues found on its pages: violence, rape, ethnic pride, tribalism, schisms, economic injustice, abuses of political and religious power, exploitation of others, greed, grabbing and abusing the land, among others."

It appears to me once again that we should embrace a both-and rather than an either-or approach to our reading of Scripture. We are instructed as to character formation and personal piety. But we are also pointed toward the many areas of brokenness that God wishes to redeem. How can these two readings complement each other? And how can this complementariness help us to navigate the complicated, challenging issue raised above—the need to discern how to translate the general moral principles revealed in Scripture to new contemporary situations? In the following section, I will note an answer to this question that is pointed to by some of our contributors and conclude with my own response.

EVANGELICALS AS AGENTS FOR RESTORING THE KINGDOM OF GOD

Wyndy Corbin Reuschling exhorts Christians to *start with the kingdom of God*, adding that to do so would enable evangelicals to be counter-cultural agents in the United States:

> Perhaps starting with the kingdom of God as the source of our moral vision will combat the tendency to link the moral vision and ethical sensibilities of the people of God with any one nation, such as the United States . . . starting with the kingdom of God based on the trajectory of Scripture and embodied as gospel would enable evangelicals to be the counter-cultural agents they purport to be but sadly are not.

Kyle Roberts posts a similar exhortation, drawing from the writings of James McClendon,[5] that focuses on the role of narrative in Christian ethics:

5. McClendon, *Ethics*, 330.

A Future for American Evangelicalism

I find compelling McClendon's description of the task of narrative Christian ethics: It is "the discovery, understanding, and creative transformation of a shared and lived story, one whose focus is Jesus of Nazareth and the kingdom he claims . . .

Christian narrative ethics builds on the scientific understanding that all human beings inhabit a moral universe and come "pre-loaded" with moral impulses, leanings, and aversions. *We acquire and alter those moral impulses through hearing and experiencing impactful narratives.* Through evangelism and Christian discipleship, *we invite people into the story of Jesus Christ,* which has past, present, and future ramifications for understanding what "morality" is and ought to be. To be a follower of Jesus is to seek the mind of Christ, to seek justice, holiness, to love with a sacrificial love, and to *anticipate the coming kingdom of God,* in which human morality will happily submit and conform to the absolute holy, loving, will of God. In the interim, as individuals (shaped as we are by biology and everything else) and as communities of believers committed to following Jesus together, we are invited to think and pray very hard for discernment in navigating the moral universe and in constructing and reconstructing together the moral structures we inhabit. *We ought to have moments of intentional, serious reflection and self-criticism, being openhanded about what we think we know to be the case and being willing to be led by the Spirit, shaped by the life of Christ, and impelled by the coming kingdom, as we follow the Spirit and Scripture toward "biblical morality."*[6]

Note from my italicizing the emphasis on conversation and openness to the stories of others and the story of Jesus—we must listen to each other's "impactful narratives," being willing to be "self-critical" as we hear each other's stories and as we reflect on the "story of Jesus," and, most importantly in my estimation, as we are "impelled by the coming kingdom" (anticipating "the coming kingdom of God").

---

6. Italics mine.

Evangelicalism and Morality

In his response to one of our readers, Roberts speaks further about this focus on the "coming kingdom of God," explaining that "as a Christian I do believe that in the Christ-event and the Christ-story we have the summation of 'morality' (the 'fulfillment of the law'); we see the 'icon' of God in flesh. As Christians we are invited to live into that narrative towards the eschatological consummation of 'morality.'" In that light, Roberts regrets that "the 'moral exemplar' atonement theory gets short shrift in Evangelicalism."

Since my understanding of how I should live well as a Christian focuses on what I take to be my calling to "partner with God" in God's redemptive work toward an eventual full realization of the kingdom of God, I conclude this section with a summary of how I take that focus to be pivotal, connecting that with the centrality of the role of character (or our enduring attitudes), both of which, as our contributors have pointed out, are addressed in Scriptures:[7]

- God created all that is and said that it was "good" (Gen 1:31).

- Due to human sinfulness, all of creation has suffered brokenness.

- By means of the life, death, and resurrection of Jesus, all of creation will one day be perfectly restored to its original goodness (Col 1:19–20).

- In the meantime, Christians are called to "partner" with God as agents for God's restorative and redemptive purposes.

- God's restorative and redemptive purpose are broad, encompassing all of the created order, including reconciliation between people and God, justice, reconciliation and peace between individuals and groups now in conflict, flourishing of the natural creation, full knowledge of the nature of God's creation, and beauty (all of which I refer to as "restorative values").

---

7. For elaboration, see Heie, *Learning to Listen*, 28–37.

A Future for American Evangelicalism

- Christians are radically free, within boundaries,[8] to choose ways to foster restorative values in ways that reflect their unique particularities and their unique gifts and abilities.

- The endeavor to foster restorative values is a lifelong adaptive process, in which the results of my efforts to foster restorative values today will grant me insight into how I should continue to foster these values tomorrow and beyond.

- The place to start fostering restorative values today is to "have eyes to see" the needs of those around me and to respond in a redemptive manner.

- I will have "eyes to see" the needs of other if I am characterized by those enduring attitudes known as the "fruits of the Spirit"—love, joy, peace, patience, kindness, generosity, gentleness, and self-control (Gal 5:22–23).[9]

In terms used in the conversation reported on in this chapter, the "general principles" that inform my living are the "restorative values" that I believe I am called to foster. But these principles do not tell me how I should resort these values day by day. I am free to do that in ways that reflect who I am—informed, but not determined by, my understanding of how followers of Jesus lived out their faith in their particular contexts as recorded in the Scriptures and elsewhere.

In light of my understanding of the contours of what it means for me to live well as a Christian, as summarized above, it should now be clear to the reader why I chose to articulate the crucicentrism and activism characteristics of evangelical Christianity proposed by David Bebbington in a particular way in my introductory chapter:

---

8. For my reflections on "ethical boundaries," see "My Ethical Project" in Heie, "Mathematics: Freedom within Bounds," 220–24. For reflections on "tragic moral choice," especially pertaining to the issue of war, see "Tragedy, Just War, and Peacemaking" in ibid., *Learning to Listen*, 137–54.

9. The lesson of having the "eyes to see" the needs of others, or not, is brought home most forcefully in the Parable of the Good Samaritan recorded in Luke 10:25–37.

Evangelicalism and Morality

> Crucicentrism: The *reconciliation of all things* to God is made possible by the life, death, and resurrection of Jesus Christ
>
> Activism: *Christians are called to be agents for God's redemptive purposes*, partnering with God in the task of *reconciliation in all areas of life.*

But I would be delighted to have conversations with evangelicals who articulate these two evangelical characteristics in different ways.

ECCLESIAL PRACTICES

Amos Yong cautions us against invoking "blanket rules and prohibitions" on moral issues "without loving ecclesial practices."

As a provocative example, Yong makes the following suggestion as to how churches that believe homosexual behavior to be antithetical to scriptural ethical teachings should deal with homosexual people in a "missional" setting:

> I can think . . . of a multi-tiered approach to missional interaction with homosexual persons. One might be parallel to how a previous generation of missionaries responded to the issue of polygamy in especially the sub-Saharan African context. While, again, there were many types of responses, one of these suggested that rather than breaking up existing families, we had to be prepared for the long haul and simply invite converts to Christ not to perpetuate such relational ties into the next generation. It may be that our response to homosexual couples, in specific instances involving children or other tenuous relational realities, might embrace a similar approach, albeit one that insists on monogamous fidelity, at least for the present time, even while working with those involved in a pastorally sensitive way to explore the meaning of holy living and faithful discipleship for such persons seeking to growth in the grace and knowledge of God in Christ.

A Future for American Evangelicalism

RECKLESS GENEROSITY

An appropriate closing for this chapter is the following beautiful account of the "reckless generosity" of John Wilson's uncle Ed:

> In the real world, and for both good and ill, evangelicals—like all human beings—are making choices all the time, in every sphere of life, choices that are morally freighted. Consider, for instance, my uncle Ed . . . I liked riding with Uncle Ed in one of the old station wagons he invariably drove, even though I was often car-sick as we negotiated the curves on mountain roads. He was exceedingly generous in carrying on conversations with a talkative boy as if with another grown-up. But there were trade-offs. You never knew how long a day you were in for. Whenever Uncle Ed noticed a driver pulled over with signs of car-trouble or some other problem, he would stop to offer his help.
>
> Hmm. Looks like the fuel pump. Uncle Ed offered to take the driver to the nearest town where a replacement could be purchased at a reasonable price. (That might be an hour and a half away—but no worries.) And if the driver wasn't a pretty confident do-it-yourself mechanic, Uncle Ed would install the new part himself. Extra money? He didn't have any. But his time, his know-how, his good will: those he would share with a total stranger.
>
> In his openhanded, unforced helpfulness, Uncle Ed was at once exceptional and typical of many evangelicals I have known. Not all evangelicals, needless to say, are so openhanded. (I am far more leery of strangers, and far more protective of my time, than my uncle was.) But an almost reckless generosity, taking many different forms—adoption, for example—is one of the most striking moral traits of the evangelical world I've known over the course of a lifetime: our friend Karen Lynip's decades of literacy work in the Philippines, our friend Arne Bergstrom's work in disaster relief (Cambodia, Rwanda, Kosovo . . .), my wife Wendy's years as a hospice volunteer.
>
> Even more remarkable—to me, at least—is that the men and women (especially the women!) who practice

Evangelicalism and Morality

this God-inspired openhandedness rarely talk about it. It's almost as if they have read and absorbed certain passages in the gospels so deeply that they would be loath to draw attention to what they are doing.

Ben Mitchell thanks John Wilson for his inspiring story about Uncle Ed:

> Thank you, John, for reminding us that there is a whole wide world of evangelicals out there who are doing their best to follow the apostle's injunction: "If possible, so far as it depends on you, live peaceably with all" (Rom 12:18). Just as ethics is not just about dilemmas, so our "respectful conversations" should not be only about problems or disagreements. Sometimes, we might even humbly celebrate the achievements of our brothers and sisters and we might even rejoice in the fact that we agree with one another as much as we do.

Justin Barnard echoes Ben Mitchell's applause: "Over many years in the evangelical world, I've known thousands of 'Uncle Eds' . . . It would be refreshing to have a more hopeful conversation about the future of Evangelicalism and morality—one grounded in the realities of ordinary life."

Note especially the implications of these exhortations for the kind of conversations we should have about Evangelicalism and morality. It is important for evangelicals to engage in respectful conversations about their disagreements regarding difficult moral issues. But such conversations should be complemented by celebrations of the many evangelicals who, without fanfare, foster God's restorative values in the humdrum of ordinary life. The many Uncle Eds of the evangelical world have much to teach us.

6

Evangelicalism and Politics

Wyndy Corbin Reuschling asserts that "*finding common ground which can lead to a shared common good* . . . is an essential aspect of the purpose of politics," adding, "this notion of the common good may be a stretch for some evangelicals."[1]

Despite the "stretch for some evangelicals" that Corbin Reuschling alludes to, Amy Black asserts that "political participation provides a way—not the only way, but an important one nonetheless—for Christians to live out the great commandments to love the Lord our God with our heart, soul, mind, and strength and to love our neighbors as ourselves. Given the *possibilities to serve the common good*, evangelicals should participate in government, educate themselves on political issues, and advocate for policies they think best."[2]

I will eventually consider the issues of whether evangelicals should heed Black's exhortation to participate in politics, as well as whether this is a "stretch for some evangelicals," as suggested by Corbin Reuschling. But for now, I want to simply indicate my strong agreement with their common focus on the purpose of politics being to identify and serve a "common good." Virtually identical to

1. Italics mine.
2. Italics mine.

Evangelicalism and Politics

the assertion of Corbin Reuschling, I embrace the proposition that *the purpose of politics is to seek common ground for the common good*.[3] If we accept this statement of the purpose of politics, then the current state of politics is dismal, both as to the substance and the mode of engagement that characterizes contemporary political discourse.

As far as the substance of political discourse is concerned, the idea that politicians are seeking common ground that may lead to the common good seems quaint, if not ludicrous, these days. In listening to politicians and political pundits, it is rare to hear any mention of the quest for common ground or reference to the common good. What I mostly hear is what is "good for me" (in the quest for election) or what is good for "my party" or my particular self-interest group. This lack of vision for a common good is fed by enormous amounts of money expended by self-interest groups. With some notable exceptions, self-interest seems to reign supreme.

This promotion of self-interest creates a vitriolic mode of political engagement. I find it painful to listen to politicians talking to or about one another. Personal attacks are rampant. Too many political opponents revel in demonizing one another and impugning each other's motives. They often listen only to an echo of themselves, holding to fixed positions with little openness to learning from those with whom they disagree.

There has to be a better way to conduct politics. How should Christians respond to this dismal current state of political discourse? Are Christians part of the problem or do they have the potential to offer a solution, to model a better way? In broad terms, Christians have adopted one of the following strategies relative to political discourse: withdrawal, domination, or engagement. I will consider these strategies in turn.

---

3. For reflections on "the Common Good as Political Norm," see Skillen, *Good of Politics*, 136–41.

A Future for American Evangelicalism

CHRISTIANS WITHDRAWING FROM DIRECT POLITICAL ENGAGEMENT IN FAVOR OF PERCEIVED BETTER ALTERNATIVES

In his set of leading questions, Rob Barrett asks, "Should evangelicals form counter-cultural communities that are disengaged from the political process in order to display an attractive alternative way of life?"

As noted by Amos Yong, some streams of Evangelicalism have chosen an "alternative witness" to active involvement in "politics as usual," which can, nevertheless, be construed as an "alternative politics"[4]:

> The Radical Reformation and its legacy bequeathed a powerful vision of "political Christianity," which locates the political activity of Christ-followers not first and foremost, or even at all, within the machinery of the state, but as embodying an ecclesiological vision of what Anabaptist and Mennonite theologians have called an "alternative politics." The church living out its discipleship under Christ provides a witness to alternative construals of life in the public square.

While calling for the direct involvement of Christians in local politics, Ben Mitchell presents a compelling case for another possible alternative to direct involvement in politics at the national level in his "Call to Civil Society."[5] Noting the conviction of America's Founding Fathers that "the foundation of democracy requires a virtuous citizenry," Mitchell encourages Christians to "invest in . . . the 'seedbeds of virtue,' those institutions of American life where

---

4. See Yoder, *Politics of Jesus*. The way in which Yoder envisions the witness of Christian communities as still being a form of politics, albeit an "alternative" to direct engagement in government sponsored politics, is as follows: "The church must be a sample of the kind of humanity within which, for example, economic and racial differences are surmounted. Only then will she have anything to say to the society that surrounds her about how those differences must be dealt with" (ibid., 154). This "saying of something to society" in indeed a political expression, but it is not expressed by "government sponsored" political means.

5. Drawing on Blankenhorn and Elshtain, *Call to Civil Society*.

Evangelicalism and Politics

the seeds of virtue are planted, watered and germinated." Mitchell lists the following as some of those institutions (commonly referred to as "mediating institutions"[6]) "where we should invest our time, money and energy."

- The family
- The local community or neighborhood
- Faith communities and religious institutions
- Voluntary civic organizations
- The arts and art institutions
- Local government
- Systems of primary and secondary education
- Higher education
- Business, labor, and economic institutions
- Media institutions

Mitchell commends such investments in local institutions as "contributing to the common good" and as enabling Christians to "build the collateral to speak into public spaces as fellow citizens, not as outsiders," saying:

> Through contributing to the common good, cultivating the virtues of the resurrected life, and investing in people in our communities, we demonstrate neighbor love and the fear of God. Might there be reasons for a prophetic witness? Of course. And God calls some to be prophets like Martin Luther King Jr., to preach national repentance. But on any given day, evangelicals should be (and very often are) found serving their local communities by honoring others and planting, watering, and cultivating those seedbeds of virtue. In this way, we contribute to human flourishing as we build the collateral to speak into public spaces as fellow citizens, not as outsiders. We do so, not to instrumentalize others, but because it's just the right thing to do.

---

6. See Berger and Neuhaus, *To Empower People*.

A Future for American Evangelicalism

Mitchell does not appear to strictly preclude Christians' engagement in national politics, since the "collateral" built up by engagement in local politics could conceivably open doors for engagement in the "public space" of national politics. Others may argue that Christians should stick to local politics. In any case, local politics appears to be a good place to start.

Here is my personal take on all of the above. Given my general aversion to either-or thinking and my attraction to both-and thinking, I embrace both strategies of modeling alternative ways of living in our Christian communities as well as direct participation in politics and other institutions of civil society, as long as their proponents don't make exclusive claims for these strategies. In other words, I certainly believe that Christians need to model alternative ways of living in their faith communities. But, for me, that should be in addition to, not in place of, Christians' direct involvement in politics and other institutions of civil society.

That is not to say that any one Christian can invest in all of these means of "witness." Each Christian must choose to make those investments that best fit his or her gifts and abilities. And it is unbiblical to think that some of these forms of Christian witness are more important than others, since the clear biblical teaching is that God's restorative intentions for creation are fostered by the collective body of Christians planting seeds of redemption, with each Christian contributing according to his or her giftedness and particular sense of calling.[7]

By now my reason for embracing this comprehensive view of our Christian witness in the world should be obvious. As I have already said a number of times, I believe that God intends to restore all of creation, not just selected aspects of creation, through Jesus Christ. And that includes redeeming the political order at both the local and national level (recall my articulations of Bebbington's evangelical characteristics of crucicentrism and activism).

Of course, some Christians may want to appeal to the projected "effectiveness" of some initiatives as compared to others. For example, there may be some in certain streams of Evangelicalism

---

7. See 1 Cor 12.

who believe that current political discourse, local or national, is so broken that modeling an alternative way of living is the only "effective" witness. I totally reject that line of thinking. Nothing is beyond some measure of redemption.

Consideration also needs to be given to what would be missing in the political arena if there were no religious voices. Randall Balmer's assessment is that "political discourse would be impoverished without . . . voices of faith." So it is that I, along with Balmer and others among my contributors, firmly believe that Christians need to seek to plant seeds of redemption in the political process, despite or because of its current brokenness. But some evangelicals have carried that conviction to lengths that have proven destructive to God's intention for the political realm, a topic to which I now turn.

CHRISTIANS SEEKING TO DOMINATE POLITICAL DISCOURSE

Rob Barrett posed the following leading question: "How far should evangelicals seek to shape the broader culture through political action in order to achieve *its own vision for living rightly with God*?"[8]

Every human being who has a strong commitment to a particular view of what it means for *all* humans to "live rightly" (whether in light of a belief in God or some other "ultimate reality") will hope that the broader culture will embrace that particular view. So, it is not unusual that Christians would try to persuade all others of the cogency of their Christian "vision for living rightly with God." But it is another question as to whether Christians should seek to impose their particular vision for "living rightly" on those who do not share their Christian faith. This is tantamount to asking whether Christians should dominate political discourse.

Randall Balmer answers with a resounding "no" when he asserts, "when evangelicals talk about participating in public discourse, we must be careful to understand that that participation

8. Italics mine.

does not mean domination." Rather, political participation (in America) "means adding our voices to a conversation governed by the canons and traditions of democracy—and, in turn, respecting other voices," especially minority voices.

Balmer grounds his assertion in the First Amendment to the Constitution of the United States, saying, "The beauty of the First Amendment is that it set up a free marketplace for religion in the United States. No one religion enjoys state sanction, and all religions must compete in this marketplace."

Granting that evangelicals disagree about the supposed "Christian origins" of the United States,[9] American society is currently characterized by a high degree of pluralism in terms of visions for "living rightly" among its diverse citizenry. No one such vision should be given a privileged voice in political discourse, which clearly precludes the notion that Christians (or any other religious or secular subgroup) should dominate such discourse.[10] As I and other evangelicals have said, "political discourse should take place on an even playing field."[11]

Problems Created by Efforts at Domination and Other Political Misadventures of Evangelicals

Another leading question posed by Rob Barrett is: "What have been the effects, both positive and negative, and both on the church and the broader society, of recent evangelical political movements?"

I hardly know where to begin to chronicle the "negative effects" mentioned by many of our contributors. For starters, John Hawthorne suggests that "many in the church ... [have] adopted special-interest tactics," leading to the worry that "the body of Christ would be seen as simply another advocacy group." If the

---

9. See Fea, *Christian Nation*.

10. Such "principled pluralism" has been advocated for many years by the Center for Public Justice (CPJ). See Skillen, *Recharging*, and Skillen and McCarthy, *Political Order*.

11. See Monsma, *Positive Neutrality*, and Monsma and Soper, *Equal Treatment*.

Evangelicalism and Politics

prominence of special-interest groups is a major defect in current political discourse, then evangelicals need to avoid being perceived as "just another one of those self-interested groups."[12]

Karl Giberson expresses this concern much more strongly when he asserts that evangelicals have been co-opted by "powerful interests, many of whom care nothing about faith," concluding with a provocative list of many viewpoints to which he believes "most evangelicals have signed on":

> Powerful interests, many who care nothing about faith, have managed to make abortion and gay marriage the only truly important issues for Christians. And then, somehow, they have mysteriously attached the following issues, and most evangelicals have signed on, thinking the whole package is uniformly Christian:
>
> 1) Growing wealth inequality is fine.
>
> 2) The free market allocates wealth fairly.
>
> 3) Taxes are bad.
>
> 4) Government is bad, except for waging war.
>
> 5) Social justice is stealing money from "makers" and giving it to "takers."
>
> 6) Universal healthcare is bad.
>
> 7) Poverty is acceptable, since Jesus said there will "always" be poor people.
>
> 8) Massive wealth concentrated in the hands of a few people is not a problem.
>
> 9) Corporations are good and don't need government regulations to make them behave in socially responsible ways.

It is certainly debatable as to whether "most evangelicals" have "signed on" to these positions, as asserted by Giberson. But I know a number of evangelicals who embrace a number of these

---

12. The idea of evangelicals being "just another one of those self-interested groups" is clearly antithetical to the teaching in Rom 12:2 that Christians should not be "conformed to this world."

positions. To the extent that this may be the case, I view that as a negative effect of some recent evangelical political movements.

Another prominent theme a number of our contributors posted on regarding the negative effects of some recent evangelical political movements is the manner in which many evangelicals have allowed themselves to be drawn into partisanship. Ted Williams says that "unfortunately, the Christian community, *lacking a true alternative,* finds itself forced to take sides in overly simplified, partisan ideological battles."[13]

A devastating effect of being forced to "take sides" with one political party in this way is that evangelicals are then drawn into the ways in which the major political parties frame debates. As Williams says, "America's two major political parties frame our debates in ways that falsely demonize and isolate those with different opinions." My own view is that Christians are being drawn into a form of debate that is antithetical to the Christian faith—but more about that later.

In light of this problem of partisanship, Kurt Anders Richardson suggests that "evangelicals should become a little indifferent to political parties and rather vote their consciences as best they can." Most tellingly as a prelude to things to come in this chapter, Richardson calls for a "national conversation" in politics that is "not about party affiliation, but about truth and charity."

In a similar vein, Jeannine Brown expresses concern that our "political allegiances" may unduly reflect our "advantages and privileges as US citizens" in that "we should take a close look at our political allegiances, asking ourselves if we've capitulated to our advantages and privileges as US citizens instead of reflecting theologically (christologically) on our loyalties." Wyndy Corbin Reuschling echoes Brown's concern, referring to the "possibility that national citizenship and Christian commitments may actually conflict at times."

Kyle Roberts seconds Brown's concern about the absence of adequate theological reflection, calling into question an "escapist eschatology" that "works well for those of us who have it pretty

---

13. Italics mine.

good" by pointing out that "conservative evangelicals too often are escapist in our eschatology: this life is a blip on the radar screen; a temporary dwelling place, so inferior to our eternal home that it's not much worth caring about or investing in."

In contrast to escapism, Roberts call evangelicals to a "*continualist* eschatology [that] . . . brings us closer to the mind of the biblical prophets, whose eschatological vision was viscerally physical (see Isa 11, for example). Like the Hebrew prophets, Jesus' vision of salvation and of the kingdom was embodied, concrete, and visceral. It involved food, freedom, and a healed creation."

Another problem with recent evangelical forays into politics is an undue focus on what we are "against" rather than what we are "for." John Hawthorne suggests that this explains the Barna Group data on "millennials leaving the church," observing that "at least some of the disaffection of today's young people comes from seeing church leaders as overly strident on social issues, being anti-science, anti-homosexual. In short, it's about being known for what one is against and not what one is for."[14]

It should be noted that it is not just certain evangelicals who focus on what they are "against" rather than what they are "for." When politicians want to repeal existing laws without replacing them with better laws, they have succumbed to the same defect.

The above narrative from our contributors does not paint a rosy picture of any positive effects of evangelicals' recent political involvements, especially those evangelicals who seek to dominate the political landscape. This leads Wyndy Corbin Reuschling to ask, "Can we conceive of more faithful ways of being Christians without the expectation that we should 'get our way'?"

Two of our contributors point us toward a better way for Christians to engage in politics. Amy Black asserts the "the problem [for Evangelicalism] is not political engagement in and of itself; the problem is that many Christians fail to demonstrate Christ-like character as they engage in politics," adding that "evangelicals should participate in politics as an act of Christian love,

---

14. See Barna Group, "The Barna Millennials Project," *Barna.org*, https://www.barna.org/barna-update/millennials.

but they should do so in a manner that demonstrates the fruit of the Spirit and with awareness of the limits of politics."[15]

Consistent with his focus on calling Christians to embrace a "continualist eschatology," Kyle Roberts calls Christians to seek to conform their political activity to "the greater purposes of God for creation." Roberts writes, "As any evangelical will affirm, only God can—and will—bring about the kingdom. Social and political action by human agency and imagination cannot and will not usher it in. But there is no reason we should not begin to think a little harder about the ways in which our political involvements (or lack thereof) connect to the greater purposes of God for creation."

Black and Roberts' suggestions hint at a better way for evangelicals to engage in politics than many of their recent endeavors. But before my contributors and I flesh out this better way, I present a brief detour that highlights even further the need for a better way.

THE INEVITABILITY OF CHRISTIANS DISAGREEING IN THE POLITICAL REALM

John Hawthorne hints that Christian disagreement in the political realm may be inevitable when he notes the difference between "what is scriptural priority (to some eyes) and what makes for public policy solutions."

What makes this difference crucial is the distinction between "means" and "ends" highlighted by Amy Black. She first asserts that "the Bible isn't an instruction manual on public policy. Instead, it teaches principles and narrates paradigms that apply to all of life, including politics." She then provides the following examples in which agreed-upon "ends" do not lead to agreement about the most desirable "means" for accomplishing those ends: "There is widespread agreement that poverty is bad, a strong economy is good, and peace is preferable to war. But even in areas of widespread agreement like these, views diverge significantly on how

---

15. More about these "limits" later.

to achieve agreed-upon goals and what tradeoffs are acceptable to achieve political agreement."

Why is there so much disagreement as to desired "means" when "ends" are readily agreed upon? Two of our contributors propose that it is due to differences in our social locations. Ted Williams reports that "studies have . . . shown that most churchgoing Americans arrive at political positions primarily consistent with their socioeconomic status, ethnic affiliation, gender, and geographic location," the result being that "what we believe and profess on Sunday morning is often separate from how we engage in the political process and culture on Monday."

Christine Kim concurs with Williams:

> The empirical data suggests that, while certain dimensions of religiosity—religious attendance, religious beliefs, religious affiliation—are sometimes correlated with some of our political attitudes and behaviors, other non-religious factors (our gender, education, geographic residency, socio-economic status, etc.) are often better at predicting these outcomes, even among evangelicals.

In the following extended quotation, Corwin Smidt eloquently points out the following additional factors that inevitably lead to Christian disagreement over political initiatives: humankind's sinful condition; the fact that the Bible does not explicate a particular philosophical perspective related to civic and political matters; differing beliefs relative to the likely consequences (both intended and unintended) of governmental actions; and the moral ambiguity associated with politics and policymaking, due in part to the complexity of the problems politics must deal with, about which our information is always incomplete. As Smidt writes:

> Human thought is always tainted by the adverse effects of the fall and humankind's sinful condition. And, as a result, neither the political left nor the political right can claim the mantel of divine favor . . . Certainly, the Protestant tradition within the Christian faith has long advanced the notion of *sola Scriptura* as the basis for discerning God's will for humankind. But when we seek

A Future for American Evangelicalism

to apply the principle of *sola Scriptura* for guiding our political thinking about politics, there are . . . complications in doing so . . . First, given the purposes for which it was written, the Bible does not provide any substantial, systematical discussion of politics that explicates a particular philosophical perspective related to civic and political matters . . . Moreover, factors other than one's theological perspectives come into play with regard to interpreting biblical texts. In addition to possible theological differences, there are also likely to be differences among Christians in terms of the analytical understandings of such principles of justice, the common good, and equality. For example, even if all Christians could agree that the state should pursue justice, it is far from clear just what that might mean, as there are different analytical understandings as to whether justice is retributive, distributive, or restorative in nature.

Finally, assessments related to the role of government are also related to other, more empirically related, factors. For example, such assessments are also likely to be shaped by: one's interpretation of the proscribed powers given by the American constitution to different levels of government; one's assessments of the present cultural, social, and economic realities within American life; one's judgment related to the root causes of problems that are currently confronting American society; and one's beliefs related to the likely consequences (both intended and unintended) of governmental actions.

Given these differences in theological understandings, analytical perspectives, and empirical assessments, it is not surprising that Christians who endeavor to be faithful to their Christian calling and who also seek to be faithful to Scripture can easily come to different views related to the role and function of government, the particular political priorities or issues to be addressed, the specific public policies that should be pursued related to such political priorities, and the political party most likely to pursue and implement such policies. . . . [Another] basis for the exercise of political civility in politics is the moral ambiguity associated with politics and policymaking . . . there are three facets about the nature of politics

Evangelicalism and Politics

that contribute to its moral ambiguity. First, politics frequently relates to choosing between relative goods in terms of political ends, and the moral ambiguity of politics relates to the need to decide which of these various relative political goods are more substantial, meritorious, or critical in nature than other such goods.

A second characteristic of politics that contributes its moral ambiguity relates to the very complicated problems with which politics must deal. Not only are many political problems immensely complex, but decisions related to these complex issues must almost always be forged on the basis of incomplete, inadequate, and/or ambiguous information.

The inevitable disagreement among Christians regarding political issues destroys the myth, too often promulgated by the media, that there is a monolithic Christian or evangelical voice. In one of his leading questions, Rob Barrett observes that "there are evangelical political movements that lean 'right' and others that lean 'left,'" asking, "Does it make sense that evangelicals publicly advocate different political positions? Is this healthy?" My resounding answers are "yes" and "yes," provided evangelicals can model for the all of America that respectful conversations about their disagreements can bear positive political fruit, which leads to my substantive proposal.

PROPOSED MODE FOR CHRISTIAN ENGAGEMENT IN POLITICS

Having rejected both the "withdrawal" and "domination" strategies relative to Christians participating in politics, I concur with proposals from a number of my contributors for a form of active engagement that differs radically from the prevalent forms of political discourse on the part of both Christians and others, as follows.

Amy Black powerfully exhorts Christians to "model a better way" for doing politics than current prevalent political discourse, a mode of engagement characterized by such virtues as humility,

A Future for American Evangelicalism

kindness, patience, and generosity, and a commitment to "speaking the truth in love." Black writes:

> When evangelicals get involved in politics, they can lose sight of their ultimate goal to love God and neighbor, focusing instead on their own self interests. At their worst, Christian political movements become triumphalist and power-seeking; their leaders are arrogant, contentious, and condescending. At their best, however, Christian political movements can offer a powerful witness of Christ's upside-down kingdom, modeling humility, grace, and repentance in the public square.

Almost every aspect of the current political climate runs counter to biblical values. Politicians and commentators tend to exaggerate and distort the facts to make political points or entertain an audience. The tone of most political communication is boastful and arrogant; the goal is often to tear down and attack opponents. Social media and the blogosphere abound with comments full of vitriol, spite, and hate.

Christians are far from immune. Some prominent activists on the evangelical left and right speak and act as if they know the mind of God on arcane political matters, explicitly or implicitly communicating that those who disagree with them are on the side of evil. So much of what happens in the political realm seems to fit the Apostle Paul's description of the works of the flesh in Gal 5, a list that includes strife, jealousy, anger, quarrels, dissensions, factions, and envy.

Evangelicals have an opportunity to model a different approach. In politics, as in all spheres of life, we should seek to honor God in word and deed. Instead of mirroring the values of the world, Christians are called to demonstrate the fruit of the Spirit: love, joy, peace, patience, kindness, generosity, faithfulness, gentleness, and self-control. We rarely see such characteristics modeled in contemporary politics as they run counter to the expected "rules of the game."

Consider the radical dimensions of God's love outlined in 1 Cor 13: "Love is patient; love is kind; love is not envious or boastful or arrogant or rude. It does not insist on its own way; it is not irritable or resentful; it does not rejoice in wrongdoing, but rejoices in the truth. It bears all things, believes all things, hopes all things, endures all things." A robust, Christ-centered politics is an extension of this powerful love; it shifts the focus from self to others, pointing the way to God's truth with humility and kindness.

Christians can choose humility over arrogance, disagree but remain gracious, and speak the truth in love. Following such principles is not a formula for worldly success, but it is a way to be faithful witnesses for Christ.

Other contributors echo Black's exhortation. John Hawthorne says that "we'll need to find better ways of engaging with those who do not share our faith perspectives," adding that this "will require much patience, careful listening, and far less pronouncing."

Christine Kim says that "when engaging in political discourse or action in the public square or in a Christian community, my attitude and posture should be that of humility and civility; I do not presume to have the right answer just because I hold an 'evangelical perspective.'"

Sarah Ruden laments the "political polarization within Christianity," and suggests that "we might . . . achieve more clarity by considering the ingrained ways we react to controversy and interact with each other as controversy plays out, in contrast to the habits of the more-peaceful early propagators of Christianity," then elaborating with the example set by the Apostle Paul.

Corwin Smidt also presents a clarion call for civility, charity, and respect when engaging in politics with those with whom we disagree:

> Finally, the third basis for exercising greater civility in politics is that, given the biblical command to love one's neighbor as oneself, it is imperative that Christians be willing to exercise greater charity to one's political opponents. With its competing values, policy priorities, and social and economic assessments related to policy-making, politics always entails the presence of disagreement. But, one of the most important decisions we as

Christians can make related to politics is the manner by which we choose to treat those with whom we disagree.

There is clearly a need for greater civility and charity in contemporary American political life. On the one hand, there are practical reasons to do so. But there are important religious reasons to do so as well. We must treat those with whom we disagree politically with respect because of who they are. Though we may disagree strongly with others, we must never forget they are image-bearers of God and thereby possess inherent dignity and right of conscience. We are to treat others with respect and good manners regardless of their political perspectives. When we treat our political opponents with disdain, we publicly dishonor God.

The fact that our political opponents are image-bearers of God and that we are commanded to love our neighbors as ourselves should be sufficient enough to cause us as Christians to treat our political opponents with civility and respect—regardless of who they may be, the particular policies they may propose, or the particular religion, or lack thereof, which they exhibit or express. But, not only do we as Christians frequently fail to do so, we all too often judge and treat our fellow brothers and sisters in Christ on the basis of the political positions they adopt. Somehow we come to view other Christians who do not hold the political positions we do as either exhibiting a "less informed faith in Christ" or even "not a true faith in Christ." In other words, we let our political and ideological perspectives make judgments about the nature of someone else's faith in Christ, forgetting that we not the ones who are to separate the sheep from the goats.

Smidt's call for civility, charity, and respect when engaging in politics is based on his understanding of what it means to "love one's neighbor as oneself." I concur wholeheartedly. It is my belief that a deep expression of what it means to love another person is to provide him or her a safe, welcoming space to disagree on important issues, political or otherwise, and to then engage in respectful conversation about such disagreements, thereby opening up the potential for mutual learning.

I'VE SEEN RESPECTFUL POLITICAL DISCOURSE MODELED WITH MY OWN EYES

Prompted by my utter dismay at the pathetic state of contemporary political discourse, I hosted an "Alternative Political Conversation" (APC) on my website, www.respectfulconversation.net, for the nine-month period from February through October 2012.

During this electronic conversation (eCircle), six evangelical Christians (including Amy Black) who situated themselves all along the political spectrum from "left" to "right" posted position papers on each of twelve pre-announced public policy issues[16] at three-week intervals. Readers were able to submit comments on the postings by the six primary contributors in a moderated forum.

The stated purpose of this eCircle was to "model respectful conversation between evangelical Christians who disagree about important public policy issues." I believe that a careful reading of these postings will reveal that this purpose was accomplished to an admirable degree. First, the conversations were indeed respectful. Contributors holding to some strong disagreements about controversial issues demonstrated a deep level of respect for those with whom they disagreed. Contrary political opinions were expressed with deep conviction without calling into question the integrity or motives of those who disagreed.

Secondly, we demonstrated that when people who situate themselves at various points on the political spectrum respectfully share their positions on difficult public policy issues, it is possible to identify some common ground in the midst of their differences and to illuminate their differences in a way that opens the door to the possibility of continuing the conversation.

---

16. See n. 1, p. 51 for a listing of the public policy issues.

A Future for American Evangelicalism

As a follow-up to the eCircle, I published a book[17] that featured "synthesis essays" on each of the public policy issues, with each essay summarizing common ground (or "majority opinion") for my contributors and "Questions for Further Conversation" (reflecting either unresolved disagreements or aspects of the issue at hand that the contributors did not address). The six contributors then concluded the book with individual essays focusing on future possibilities for respectful conversations in the political realm.

So, it can be done, and it has been done. This group of deeply committed evangelicals has exemplified openness to respectfully listening to other evangelicals who disagree with them on controversial public policy issues and engaging them in respectful conversation. It is my hope and prayer that in the days to come this model will be replicated by many evangelicals who want to exemplify a "better way" to do politics.

For those evangelicals who wish to limit political engagement in politics to the "alternative politics" of a witness within Christian communities because of the "brokenness" of government-sponsored politics,[18] I propose that my APC project can be viewed as a model of a way by which Christians can become directly involved in political discourse without participating in the brokenness of "politics as usual." Of course it can be argued that my APC and subsequent book reporting on the results of this online conversation will likely have little effect on the broken world of contemporary politics. But I believe I am called to be "faithful" to my Christian faith, even if that does not translate into effectiveness.

THE NEED FOR BALANCE AND BIPARTISANSHIP IN POLITICS

Recall the concern expressed in an earlier chapter that the polarization among many evangelicals reflects erroneous either-or thinking that fails to strike an appropriate balance between private

---

17. See Heie, *Evangelicals on Public Policy Issues*.
18. See n. 4, p. 70.

and ecclesial efforts to assist the poor and the efforts of government or a balance between individual morality and social morality. Another type of balance is now called for.

A recurring theme throughout the twelve conversations on my APC eCircle was the need for balance between competing views on various public policy issues. Here is my summary of the conclusions reached by the contributors to that conversation:

> There is little hope for solving the Federal Budget Deficit problem unless a balance is struck between the need for cuts in expenditures and the need for increased revenues.
>
> Those debating the immigration issue must balance the call for improved border protection and punishment of those who have entered our country illegally with the pressing need to provide a viable pathway to citizenship for those undocumented workers who are making an enormous contribution to our economy and our country and whose families are being decimated by current immigration laws.
>
> The seemingly intractable conflict between Israel and Palestine has no hope of a solution unless it is recognized that the only viable solution will need to treat both Israelis and Palestinians "justly" (enabling both peoples to flourish). As in all attempts to achieve a proper balance, either-or solutions will not work; both-and solutions are required.
>
> In the debate on healthcare, it is not only a matter of providing healthcare for many who have been uninsured. That need must be balanced by the need to reduce the spiraling costs of healthcare.
>
> The current debates regarding K-12 education need to strike a balance between the importance of providing "freedom for entrepreneurial innovation" and regulations that will avoid some expressions of such freedom to harm certain segments of our society.
>
> In the gun control debate, the choice is not between either addressing the mental health and "culture of violence" problems that beset our nation or legislatively

enacting some common sense gun control measures. It has to be both.[19]

The quest for such balance relative to public policy legislation is wishful thinking in the hyper-partisan milieu of contemporary politics, where the reigning rule of thumb is "it's my way or the highway." One step toward overcoming this lack of balance would be for people on both sides of the political aisle to be willing to give serious consideration to the "best ideas" of those on the other side in an effort to forge bipartisan legislation.[20] This will require respectful conversations across the aisle.

Of course, engaging in respectful conversation with political opponents will not solve the severe structural problems in politics that fuel the prevailing disrespect. Our current political system rewards those who hold to extreme "my way or the highway" positions, largely through the huge amounts of money donated to those holding to extreme positions, which punishes those who desire to "govern from the middle." These structural problems will not be solved anytime soon. Therefore, there is little political incentive

---

19. Ibid., 140–41.
20. Michael A. King gives radical expression to the ideal of giving serious consideration to the "best ideas of those on the other side" in his "summary of genuine conversation," saying: "I have come to summarize genuine conversation as involving a mutual quest for treasure in our own and the other's viewpoint. This entails making two key moves. The first move is 'to make as clear as I can why I hold this position [prejudice] and why you might find in it treasure to value in your own quest for truth.' The second key move is 'to see the value in the other's view [prejudice] and to grow in my own understandings by incorporating as much of the other's perspective as I can without losing the integrity of my own convictions,'" (King, "Conversations," 153). In response to King's proposal as to what constitutes a "genuine conversation," Carolyn Schrock-Shenk asserts that openness to "changing one's perspective or conviction about an issue" is "rarely realistic, especially in relation to issues as charged as homosexuality." Rather, she proposes that "a minimum requirement for genuine dialogue is a readiness to change or modify one's perspective about *the person or persons* holding the opposite point of view" (qtd. in King, *Stumbling*, 15). Even that more limited ideal would be a major accomplishment when dealing with public policy issues and the controversial social issues that are currently tearing some churches and religious denominations apart.

Evangelicalism and Politics

to engage in respectful conversation across the aisle. But, from a Christian perspective, it is the right thing to do.

A HIGH PRIORITY AGENDA FOR CHRISTIAN POLITICAL ENGAGEMENT

John Hawthorne asserts that "evangelicals are at our best when we're advocating for those who can't advocate for themselves," adding that this "means that we are passionate about justice—not just in a narrow partisan sense but in the 'least of these' sense. Let's worry less about political party orientation and think together with non-evangelicals about how we speak on behalf of those without voice: The poor, the broken, the abandoned, the hurting, the addicted, the dispirited."

Justin Barnard concurs in his assertion that "a fully-orbed vision of the kingdom includes the extension of creational fecundity to the poor and marginalized, 'the widow and the orphan.'" Randall Balmer strikes a similar note about the need for evangelicals to focus on the "well being of those on the margins of society," which he finds lacking in recent evangelical political advocacy. He writes:

> As I argue in my forthcoming biography of Jimmy Carter,[21] the 1970s saw a brief efflorescence of progressive Evangelicalism, a tradition informed by the teachings of Jesus to care for "the least of these" and that flourished in the nineteenth and early twentieth centuries. These evangelicals of an earlier era, from Charles Grandison Finney to William Jennings Bryan, directed their energies to the well being of those on the margins of society—slaves, women, immigrants, prisoners, the poor—a disposition that I find conspicuously absent in recent evangelical political advocacy. There are exceptions, of course, but I regard the sentiments of the 1973 Chicago Declaration of Evangelical Social Concern and the policies of evangelicals like Hatfield, Hughes, and

21. Balmer, *Redeemer*.

Carter as far more consistent with both the New Testament and with the noble legacy of nineteenth-century Evangelicalism.

In light of his belief that "the clearest teaching of the Bible . . . is concern for the poor," Karl Giberson expresses his dismay about Christians who "think Ayn Rand comports with their faith," when she was a "philosopher of selfishness," and "an unambiguously anti-Christian thinker who celebrated selfishness and condemned charity."

These strong assertions by a number of contributors clearly comport with the primacy of concern for "the least of these" in our society, which Jesus taught in Matt 25, and points to the need for the future political agenda for evangelicals to focus on the most needy in our midst who are virtually voiceless in the political process.

THE LIMITS ON POLITICAL ACCOMPLISHMENT

Wyndy Corbin Reuschling asks the probing questions: "What can we reasonably expect from our political systems? Do we practice a form of idolatry by assuming too much from our political involvement and from political processes?"

Amy Black responds that "evangelicals should participate in politics . . . with awareness of the limits of politics," for the following reason (drawn from the exhortations of Mark Rodgers, a former Senate staffer):

> "Culture is upstream of politics." Politicians are much more likely to follow trends than to set them. Moving ahead of culture entails significant political risks. It is far easier—and safer—for elected officials to respond to societal change than to try and direct it. [Therefore] evangelicals can and should advocate for public policies that align with their commitments and principles. But when their beliefs run counter to the prevailing culture, they should not expect political success. The best way for evangelicals to shape the broader culture is by living

faithful lives, demonstrating the fruits of the spirit, and bearing witness to Christ in word, deed, and truth.

John Hawthorne concurs with Black's exhortation to bear Christian witness when he says that "the secret to political engagement, it seems to me, is that we are called to witness to that kingdom *even if we lose the argument*. Maybe especially then. Consider Wilberforce and the decades-long fight over slavery."

But as Dan Knauss notes in a response to Hawthorne, such bearing of Christian witness in the political realm, without assurance of success, runs counter to the penchant of evangelicals to "want the whole loaf or nothing, and to label those willing to settle for 'a half loaf' as 'sellouts.'" Knauss explains:

> For many Evangelicals it is an existential threat to be told they must swallow hard and work with people who do not share all their principles in the hope of gaining a half loaf rather than none at all. There is something within Evangelicalism and nearly all minorities that would rather lose all on their own and be right all to themselves ... I do not know how one might go about moving more Evangelicals into this ecumenical and pragmatic state of mind. It is a task that in many contexts opens one to being attacked as a "liberal," a sellout, a wolf in sheep's clothing.

I believe that even if I gain only a "half-loaf" through political means, if that half-loaf fosters God's redemptive purposes, then I have faithfully sown some "seeds of redemption" and I can entrust the harvest to God (Matt 13:31–32).

7

Evangelicalism and Scientific Models of Humanity and Cosmic and Human Origins

AN ANTI-SCIENCE STANCE IN SOME STREAMS OF EVANGELICALISM

In his introduction to the eCircle conversation that informs this chapter, Rob Barrett puts his finger on a "significant tension" within certain streams of Evangelicalism when he observes that "recent decades have seen a solidifying scientific consensus concerning the evolutionary origin of human life over a long period of time that stands in significant tension with common readings of Gen 1–3."

Some streams of Evangelicalism have responded to this tension by rejecting the "scientific consensus concerning the evolutionary origin of human life," in particular, and, more generally, by taking an "anti-science stance." Citing the research of David Kinnaman,[1] Kyle Roberts notes that it is this "anti-science attitude"

---

1. Kinnaman, *You Lost Me*.

Evangelicalism and Scientific Models of Humanity

that causes many churched teenagers to drop out of church." As Roberts explains:

> Close to 60 percent of churched teenagers drop out of church after high school, often rejecting their faith altogether. One of the reasons for this, as Kinnaman's research shows, is a perceived "anti-science" attitude within the church. Pastors, youth pastors, and other church leaders either ignore issues raised by science or they take an aggressive stance against it.

In light of that "perceived 'anti-science' attitude within the church," Roberts goes on to suggest that "another apologetic need [other than that directed primarily to non-Christians] is arising today within the church itself. This apologetic argues that the perceived forced choice between science and faith is a false dichotomy," adding that this false dichotomy "is perpetuated by many pastors, youth pastors, and other leaders in conservative streams of Christianity."

Christopher Hays echoes the concerns expressed by Roberts, further suggesting that this false dichotomy reflects a faulty view of "Christian piety":

> Ironically, my evangelical tradition had actually hamstrung the evangelism effort by contributing to the erroneous supposition that Christianity and mainstream science are ideological alternatives. In fundamentalist circles, this anti-scientism is sometimes taken as a mark of Christian piety. But I would like to suggest the opposite: *Christian piety should motivate a far more robust engagement with mainstream science than has hitherto characterized the evangelical tradition.*

In light of this tendency towards an anti-science stance within certain streams of Evangelicalism, Kyle Roberts eloquently states the challenge facing evangelicals regarding the relationship between science and faith:

> It would not surprise me if these questions surrounding the intersection of theology and science become the next frontier of popular, evangelical debate (we're probably

already there). A number of theologians, philosophers, and scientists who are self-identifying evangelical Christians are exploring these questions and others in the pursuit toward a more integrative Christian theology and a more cohesive Christian faith. Books and academic papers are being written, grant projects are under way . . . and conferences and colloquia are taking place. Key to the sustainability of these academic projects, however, will be their translatability into the parlance of the everyday pastor and of the "Christian in the pew," many of whom have been socialized within their evangelical faith to either avoid science or to combat it. It will be important to show that this integrative work is consonant with a high view of Scripture and the primacy of Christ for salvation. It will also be important to develop and articulate a fully-orbed, progressive, evangelical theology that connects the dots between creation, sin, salvation, and the Eschaton—and which allows science to have a prominently descriptive role (one of the *strata*) in that theology. For that to happen, evangelical seminaries will need to be involved.

A first step in facing this challenge is to formulate an adequate understanding of the nature of science and religion as well as their possible interface, a topic to which my contributors and I now turn.

THE INTERFACE BETWEEN SCIENCE AND RELIGION

In his leading questions for this chapter, Rob Barrett poses the pivotal question concerning the relationship between "scientific study" and "biblical study," asking, "To what extent are these two forms of inquiry in conversation, or are they wholly separate?"

A number of our contributors assert that our Christian faith points us to a reality that goes beyond what science can explain. For example, Amos Yong says that "there are also limits to what science can discover, since it does focus on the material world.

Evangelicalism and Scientific Models of Humanity

Christian faith will always 'know' and believe more than what science will ever hope to explain. Yet what faith knows and believes cannot ultimately contradict what science independently uncovers, since all truth, as Arthur Holmes emphasized, is God's truth." In a similar vein, Peter Enns asserts, "By faith I believe that the Christian story has deep access to a reality that materialism cannot provide and cannot be expected to know." Kyle Roberts elaborates by asserting that "while science helps us to explain things at an empirical, natural level, Scripture provides explanations and insight into theological, moral, and metaphysical realities."

From my own formal education in science and subsequent reflections on the relationship between science and my Christian faith, I express the views noted above in the following way. In my role as a scientist, I can assume a "methodological naturalism." For example, scientists can predict what will typically happen in the "natural world" given certain antecedent conditions and *assuming no intervention into the natural world*. But a scientist must remain mute as to whether interventions into the natural world are possible. That is not a scientific question; it is a metaphysical question. Therefore, as a scientist who is also a Christian, I have no difficulty believing, on the basis of my metaphysical beliefs, that God can intervene in the natural world and bring about those atypicalities that we call "miracles."

To be sure, scientists can succumb to the temptation of "scientism," believing that reality is limited to that which can be explained "naturally." But that belief is not a scientific belief; it is a metaphysical belief.[2]

As Amos Yong implies, those who have embraced "scientism" have succumbed to assuming that "methodological naturalism" necessarily leads to "metaphysical naturalism," which is antithetical to the Christian faith: "Part of the challenge . . . is that the methodological naturalism that has driven scientific inquiry from

---

2. For those readers who view metaphysical beliefs as no more than personal preferences, two Christian philosophers have proposed criteria for adjudicating competing metaphysical beliefs. See Hasker, *Metaphysics*, and Wolfe, *Epistemology*.

A Future for American Evangelicalism

its early modern times is not easily disentangled from the metaphysical naturalism that is deeply problematic for Christian faith."

Therefore, in light of my understanding of the limited scope of reality that science can explain (what I call "the limitations of science"), I concur with Amos Yong's assertion that "what faith knows and believes cannot ultimately contradict what science independently uncovers." But how do I reconcile my claim that there should be no conflict between science and faith with the empirical fact that conflict among Christina regarding origins has reached epidemic proportions? As Rob Barrett noted in the opening paragraph of this chapter, the problem is that "a solidifying scientific consensus concerning the evolutionary origin of human life over a long period of time stands in significant tension with common readings of Gen 1–3."

There must be something wrong either with the "scientific consensus concerning the evolutionary emphasis of human life" or with "common readings of Gen 1–3," or both. To adequately explore these two possibilities will require much conversation between those embedded in various streams of Evangelicalism. Thankfully, these conversations are already taking place, which John Wilson, for one, finds encouraging: "The mere existence of this discussion is cheering: it couldn't have taken place when I was in high school, in the 1960s."[3] Hopefully, what follows in this chapter will provide a catalyst for such conversations to continue in a way that proves to be "positive and helpful" (which is a possibility that Rob Barrett entertains in his introduction to the eCircle conversation that informs this chapter).

But before getting into the weeds relative to some substantive issues that need to be talked about, I will reflect on some existing obstacles to continuing this conversation.

---

3. In his posting, Wilson notes the following four recent books as evidence of a "much larger ongoing dialogue" about origins: Barrett and Canaday, *Historical Adam*; Grundlach, *Process and Providence*; Stafford, *Adam Quest*; Gee, *Accidental Species*.

Evangelicalism and Scientific Models of Humanity

OBSTACLES TO A RESPECTFUL CONVERSATION ABOUT ORIGINS

Amos Yong notes the significant obstacle of "ideological biases" that are not "open to discussion and correction," observing that "the voices of unreason on both left and right will be exposed for what they are: ideologies driven by biases rather than views open to correction through public discussion and empirical data."

Peter Enns expresses concern about "a defensive, retreatist approach aimed at maintaining theological parameters deemed non-negotiable in mainstream evangelical thinking despite the evidence of science." In all fairness, a related concern at the other end of the spectrum may be a defensiveness that precludes rethinking interpretations of some of the scientific evidence despite some readings of Gen 1–3 judged to be hermeneutically responsible.

Another obstacle suggested by Kurt Anders Richardson is "the overwhelming pressure to take sides." But a somewhat unusual obstacle pointed to by two of our contributors is too strong an aversion to cognitive dissonance. From his perspective as an analytic philosopher, Justin Barnard notes that "among analytic philosophers, the threshold for genuine cognitive dissonance is quite high. Quite simply, it's logical contradiction." Therefore, "what analytic philosophers call 'prima facie' conflicts (i.e., things that appear to be in conflict 'at first glance') are not always, in the end, in the kind of deep conflict in which they initially appear."

To illustrate and to anticipate our eventual confrontation with the thorny substantive issue of the nature of "sin and death," Barnard says the following about a position taken by Peter Enns: "Enns would like me to believe that evolution makes 'claims' about the 'very nature of sin and why people die' that are at odds with Christian teaching about the same . . . 'That sure looks troubling on the face of it.' But, within a few swift strokes of analysis, I'm less perturbed" (Barnard's reasons for being "less perturbed" will be presented later in this chapter).

A Future for American Evangelicalism

Sarah Ruden calls into question our aversion to cognitive dissonance. In a posting titled "Living with Unfinished Conflict between Religion and Science," Ruden says:

> I'd just like to make the case that the evolution controversy is a phenomenon of its time, a time of environmental stress and increasing social division; much as the controversy on the origins of the Bible was fueled by rapidly increasing literacy. To think of a wound that we can trust God to heal in the fullness of time might be better than insisting that we, with our mere human abilities, can somehow work everything out and soon reach a state where there isn't considerable distress and dissonance over the issue. In fact, . . . distress and dissonance are part of the natural process, and trying to make them go away won't help and may do harm.

To add my own voice to identifying the obstacles to respectful conversations about origins, I remind readers of my assertion in the introduction to this book that a major obstacle to respectful conversation among diverse evangelicals about any contentious issue is a lack of exemplification of the Christian virtues of humility, patience, love, and courage on the part of those on both sides of the issue. An aspect of the humility that is called for is captured by the assertion of Christopher Hays that we should not "begrudge God the right to gainsay our traditional assumptions about the way he works in the world."

A GLIMPSE AT THE CURRENT DEBATE ABOUT ORIGINS

The current evangelical debate about origins is complex and nuanced. Gerald Rau has identified no less than "Six Models of the Beginning of Everything" (Naturalistic Evolution, Nontelelogical Evolution, Planned Evolution, Directed Evolution, Old-Earth Creation, Young-Earth Creation), with some Christians holding to each of the five latter positions.[4] Those who hold to Nontelelogi-

---

4. Rau, *Mapping*.

Evangelicalism and Scientific Models of Humanity

cal Evolution, Planned Evolution, or Directed Evolution are often referred to as "Evolutionary Creationists," to distinguish them from either "Old-Earth Creationists" or "Young-Earth Creationists," neither of whom believe God created through evolutionary means.

To add to the diversity of beliefs about origins, various Christians hold at least four differing views regarding "the historical Adam," which, as will soon be seen, is very much a part of the origins debate.[5]

Francis Collins poses the most critical question relative to the historicity of Adam: "Is the description of Adam's creation from the dust of the earth and the subsequent creation of Eve from one of Adams's ribs . . . a symbolic allegory of the entrance of the human soul into a previously soulless animal kingdom, or is this intended as literal history?"[6]

Although I am neither a biblical scholar nor a biologist, and may therefore now be skating on thin ice, I perceive that a major point of contention in the current debate has to do with the origin of sin and death. Those who hold to the historical Adam cite Rom 5:12–15:

> Therefore, just as sin came into the world through one man, and death came through sin, and so death spread to all because all have sinned . . . For if the many died through the one man's trespass, much more surely have the grace of God and the free gift in the grace of the one man, Jesus Christ, abounded for the many.

This biblical passage appears to clearly teach that the cause of sin and death in our world is the original sin of a historical Adam. But that does not seem to fit with the evolutionary view that "death existed before Adam and Eve's fall, since natural selection works through culling. Humanity coming late in evolutionary history,

---

5. Barrett and Canaday, *Historical Adam*.
6. Collins, *Language of God*, 206–207.

there would have been creature dying for millions of years before sin came into the world with Adam."[7]

Peter Enns, who holds to an evolutionary view of the "creation of man" and who does not believe in the historicity of Adam, expresses his view as follows in his posting on this topic:

> I argue in *The Evolution of Adam*[8] that sin and death are undeniable universal realities, whether or not we are able to attribute them to a primordial man who ate from the wrong tree. The Christian tradition, however, has generally attributed the cause to sin and death to Adam as the first human. Evolution claims that the cause of sin and death, as Paul understood it, is not viable. That leaves open the questions of where sin and death come from . . . [I]n an evolutionary scheme, death is not the enemy to be defeated. It may be feared, it may be ritualized, it may be addressed in epic myths and sagas, but death is not the unnatural state introduced by a disobedient couple in a primordial garden. Actually, it is the means that promotes the continued evolution of life on this planet and even ensures workable population numbers. Death may hurt, but it is evolution's ally.

But what, then, does Enns do with Rom 5:12,15? In brief, Enns asserts that Paul was mistaken in attributing the cause of sin and death to the disobedience of a historical Adam, writing that "Paul's understanding of Adam as the cause reflects his time and place,"[9] adding that "we are compelled to leave room for the ancient writers to reflect and even incorporate their ancient, mistaken cosmologies into their scriptural reflections."[10]

The above discussion does not adequately address the thorny question as to the cause, or lack thereof, of sin and death (Enns suggests that this must remain an open question). But it will hopefully suffice to enable me to respond to the question readers may have: Is the position that Enns takes about the evolutionary

7. Stafford, *Adam Quest*, 56.
8. See Enns, *Evolution of Adam*.
9. Ibid., 124.
10. Ibid., 95.

creation of humanity and the non-historicity of Adam acceptable as "one evangelical position?" My answer is "yes," for Enns' position does not take him outside the pale of evangelical belief, at least as understood by David Bebbington, which should open the door for respectful and fruitful conversation with other evangelicals who disagree with Enns. The basis for my positive response follows.

COMMON GROUND IN EVANGELICAL BELIEFS ABOUT ORIGINS

The above narrative focuses on certain areas of disagreement between Peter Enns and some other evangelicals, especially those who do not believe that God created by evolutionary means. But some of Enns' other writings, some of our other contributors' postings, and the writings of a few other evangelicals reveal significant common ground about origins among evangelicals who may differ on other origins issues.

For starters, Kurt Anders Richardson asserts that "the key features of creation as revealed from Scripture" are that "all things have an absolute beginning from God, who is without beginning and [is] their ultimate source." In other words, there is agreement that God exists and is the creator of our universe, even if there is disagreement as to how God created and how long it took.

Christopher Hays, in his response to a reader, asserts that "evolutionary theism" does not "amount to a denial of the universality of sin," adding that he "has never come across a Christian evolutionary theist who . . . denies the universality of sin."

John Walton, one of four contributors to the book *Four Views on the Historical Adam*, all of whom hold differing views about the historicity of Adam and Eve, believes that "Adam and Eve are historical figures . . . [yet] the biblical text is more interested in them as archetypal figures who represent all of humanity."[11] But Walton says that "we [the four contributors] all believe that people

---

11. Walton, "Historical Adam," 89.

are created by God in his image, that sin is real and we are all subject to it, and that Christ's death was necessary to resolve the sin issue."[12]

Denis Lamoureaux, another contributor to *Four Views on the Historical Adam*, denies the historicity of Adam but embraces the following "inerrant spiritual truths": "only humans are created in the Image of God, only humans have fallen into sin, and our Creator judges us for our sinfulness."[13]

And finally, in his book *The Evolution of Adam*, Peter Enns identifies the following commonalities among those who disagree about how and when God created all that is:

> I believe in the universal and humanly unalterable grip of both sin and death, and the work of the Savior, by the deep love and mercy of the Father, in delivering humanity from them ... [A]ttributing the cause of universal sin and death to a historical Adam is not necessary for the gospel of Jesus Christ to be a fully historical solution to that problem ... [T]he uncompromising reality of who Jesus is and what he did to conquer the objectively true realities of sin and death do not *depend* on Paul's understanding of Adam as a historical person.[14]

As Enns continues:

> A literal Adam may not have been the first man or the cause of sin and death as Paul understood it, but what remains of Paul's theology are three core elements of the gospel:
>
> 1. The universal and self-evident problem of death.
>
> 2. The universal and self-evident problem of sin.
>
> 3. The historical event of the death and resurrection of Christ.

---

12. Ibid., "Rejoinder," 139.
13. Lamoureux, "No Historical Adam," 37.
14. Enns, *Evolution of Adam*, xl, 82, 122.

Evangelicalism and Scientific Models of Humanity

> These three remain; what is lost is Paul's *culturally assumed* explanation for what a *primordial* man had to do with *causing* the reign of death and sin in the world. Paul's understanding of Adam as the cause reflects his place and time... The need for a savior does not require a historical Adam.[15]

The above quotations reveal that whatever differing views these evangelicals hold as to origins and the historical Adam, they all embrace the central evangelical truths that all human being are sinners who need to be redeemed by means of the death and resurrection of Jesus Christ. This focus comports with my articulation of David Bebbington's crucicentrism characteristic of Evangelicalism, which claims that "the reconciliation of all things to God is made possible by the life, death, and resurrection of Jesus Christ."

This focus also does not conflict Bebbington's evangelical characteristics of conversionism and activism, as I have articulated them here. But what about Bebbington's characteristic of biblicism? You will recall that my articulation of biblicism was:

> The Bible is true in all that it affirms; it is an authoritative account of the Christian story of creation, fall, redemption, and consummation sufficient to inform Christian faith and practice; and its truths are to be complemented by the truths about all of God's creation revealed by study in the various disciplines of knowledge.

Since my articulation of biblicism does not bypass the biblical hermeneutical task (stating that "the Bible is true in all that it affirms," which leaves open the task of interpreting what it is that each scriptural passage affirms), my view of biblicism leaves room for the scholars quoted above to disagree about the most adequate interpretations of biblical passages pertaining to origins and the historicity of Adam. Therefore, the common ground noted above can serve as starting points for ongoing conversations about their differing biblical interpretations.

15. Ibid., 123–24, 143.

A Future for American Evangelicalism

THE STATUS OF PRESENT EVANGELICAL CONVERSATIONS ABOUT ORIGINS AND A POSSIBLE FUTURE

Past conversations between evolutionary creationists and young-earth creationists have often been vitriolic. Karl Giberson recounts some painful experiences as a teacher at a Christian college because he rejected a literalistic view of biblical inerrancy that insisted on a young earth:

> Most of the students entered my classes . . . believing that evolution was the devil's lie . . . For more than two decades I had biblical inerrantists like . . . [a well known young-earth creationist] condemning me to hell and trying to get me fired for leading college students astray. I spent many long painful hours in administrator's offices dealing with these controversies, trying in vain to explain that a college education should disabuse one of the notion that the earth is 10,000 years old.

In his posting for the next subtopic, "Evangelicalism and Christian Higher Education," Giberson sadly reports that reading the comments about him at the "Reformed Nazarene" website[16] reveals comments of "people with Jesus—and hatred for fellow Christians—constantly on their lips."

But I have some good news. Evangelicals who disagree strongly about origins issues are beginning to engage one another in respectful conversations about their disagreements. For starters, there are encouraging signs that many Christians who disagree about origins issues are moving beyond the destructive past practice of calling into question the "level of Christian commitment" or the seriousness of commitment to the authority of the Bible of those who disagree with them. For example, Darrell Falk, an evolutionary creationist who believes in the historical Adam, says "We do not all have to believe the same . . . Let us not ever allow the acid

---

16. See "'Contend for the Faith' Jude 1:3," *Reformed Nazarene*, October 24, 2011, https://reformednazarene.wordpress.com/2011/10/24/arrogance-intellectual-elitism-rejection-of-scripture-karl-giberson.

Evangelicalism and Scientific Models of Humanity

test of one's Christianity to become one's view of whether Adam and Eve are figurative alone or historical *and* figurative."[17]

I am also pleased to report that in the past year I have seen with my own eyes models of respectful conversations among scholars who have strong disagreements about origins issues. These conversations, in which I have participated, have taken place in three small group face-to-face forums on origins under the auspices of The Colossian Forum (TCF), for whom I now serve as a Senior Fellow.[18]

Each of these small group forums brought together six to eight scientists and biblical scholars who had radically differing views on origins, featuring the perspectives of one young-earth creationist and one evolutionary creationist that were presented at each forum (for the most part, I was an interested observer). We read Scripture together, prayed together, and got to know one another quite well through shared meals and informal activities (e.g., a hike by the Pacific Ocean near San Diego when we met at Point Loma Nazarene University). And in that context of getting to know one another, we got beyond the all too common view that the "really committed Christians" are those who hold to a particular view on origins. We were able to talk respectfully about significant disagreements regarding origins, building on the firm foundation of mutual understanding and mutual trust that emerged from our devotional and informal times together.

The climax to our time together in San Diego was when, in our closing session, we each prayed for the person seated on our right, regardless of his or her views on origins, thanking God for that person and praying for the specific needs that we had gotten to know about during our few days together. It was an unforgettable experience that had a powerful impact on me.

What was accomplished by means of these (continuing) face-to-face forums? As far as I can tell, neither of the two featured

---

17. Stafford, *Adam Quest*, 130.

18. The mission of The Colossian Forum (TCF) in Grand Rapids, Michigan, is to create a "safe space" that "facilitates dialogue on divisive issues within the church." See www.colossianforum.org.

A Future for American Evangelicalism

presenters radically changed their beliefs about origins. But they did significantly change their beliefs about the other person, which was a huge accomplishment.

For example, the young-earth creationist changed his view that the evolutionary creationist was a "dirty, rotten compromiser" and has since committed himself to apologizing to those to whom he had presented the other scholar in that way. As a result of better understanding the substantial scientific accomplishments of the young-earth creationist, the evolutionary creationist no longer characterizes the young-earth creationist as uninformed or unable to engage the real science.[19]

The reason this change in beliefs about a person who holds differing views about origins is so important is that the level of mutual understanding and trust that has been established is the solid foundation that opens up the possibility that their ongoing conversations will enable each to refine their beliefs about origins in ways that reflect what each has learned from the other.

Although this is a great start for a new way for evangelicals who disagree with one another to respectfully engage each other, it is impossible to predict where these conversations will lead. Drawing on the work of Thomas Kuhn on the nature of "scientific revolutions,"[20] John Hawthorne holds out the tantalizing possibility of "new paradigms" emerging in our thinking about origins within both science and religion. One of our readers, Bev Mitchell, is not optimistic about this happening within the realm of religion, saying that "a good part of me wants to say that science is better prepared (sort of by its nature) to entertain the possibility of a paradigm shift." A fascinating related tidbit is that the young-earth creationist involved in the TCF forums on origins did say that he was exploring the possibility of "new paradigms."

---

19. This change in how these two scientists altered their beliefs about the other is a marvelous example of a "genuine conversation" as defined by Carolyn Schrock-Shenk (see n. 20, P. 88, quoting Schrock-Shenk: "a minimum requirement for genuine dialogue is a readiness to change or modify one's perspective about the *person or persons* holding the opposite point of view").

20. Kuhn, *Scientific Revolutions*.

Evangelicalism and Scientific Models of Humanity

While thinking about a possible future for discussions among evangelicals about origins (or other contentious issues), we do well to consider the suggestion made by Ard Louis that when dealing with complicated issues, a "communal" effort is needed, which the church has not provided.

> The real problem is that the church does not have a place for evangelical scholars to devote their lives to a very complicated subject, think about it, test it with other scholars, and eventually come to some kind of consensus. Something as complicated as evolution has scientific, biblical, historical, theological and philosophical dimensions. No one person is smart enough to solve all those things for the church. It has to be a communal thing.[21]

One immediate response to Louis's suggestion is that Christian institutions of higher education are in the best position to provide this communal venture for addressing contentious, complicated issues like origins. But, believe me, the obstacles to that dream are enormous, as we will discuss futher in the next chapter.

---

21. Louis, "Evangelical Science," 150–51.

8

Evangelicalism and Higher Education

I will frame the content of this chapter by repeating my belief that the obvious diversity within Evangelicalism is a "gift from God":

> My enthusiasm in embracing Evangelicalism's diversity as a gift from God is foundational to the message of this book. It is because I believe that those believers embedded in different streams of Evangelicalism have much to contribute to a full understanding of the Christian faith that I want each evangelical to express his or her commitments with clarity and deep conviction. At the same time, I want each evangelical to stay open to respectfully listening to and talking with those evangelicals who hold to differing beliefs and practices—the goal being that by learning from the best of each stream of Evangelicalism, we can gain a better understanding of the Truth as only God fully knows it.

Note the priority I give to the search for the Truth as only God fully knows it.

In an online conversation I once had with a good Catholic friend about the perennial tension between focusing on the "authority of the Bible" or the "authority of the Church," she asked me "where I thought 'authority' resided, if not in the Magisterium." My response then, as now, was that "I embrace the ultimate authority of Truth; not my partial understanding of the Truth as a finite, fallible human being whose beliefs are informed by my particularities; nor your partial understanding as a fellow human being; not even the teachings of the Magisterium; but Truth as only God fully knows it."[1]

This strong belief on my part that only God fully understands the Truth may not sit well with those who aspire to "certainty." I simply believe that the quest for certainty is misplaced; an aspect of the human condition, as God created us, is that we are called to live well in the midst of inevitable uncertainty.

A word needs to be said here about postmodernism. As John Hawthorne asserts, "if Christian universities don't step forward and address the issues of postmodern society, we run the risk of becoming increasingly marginalized and isolated." Postmodernism is an extremely complex movement.[2] I will limit myself here

---

1. My commitment to the "ultimate authority of truth" is not to diminish the importance of "tradition" in the Christian church. As Linda Trinkaus Zagzebski says, "If tradition is the democracy of the dead, as G. K. Chesterson observed, ignoring it is a kind of egoism of the contemporary" (Zagzebski, *Epistemic Authority*, 199). Zagzebski elaborates: "Trust in a community that has existed for many hundreds of years is often more conscientious than trusting a community of my contemporaries, and much more conscientious than trusting myself alone" (ibid., 199). By "[Epistemic] conscientiousness," she means the "self-conscious attempt to make our beliefs fit the truth" (ibid., 86). As a result, she concludes that "the self-reliant person who rejects the help of others in the task of governing herself will have a much harder time than the person who conscientiously accepts that there have always been persons wiser than herself, and the accumulated wisdom of many persons extends to beliefs, desires, and values she would do well to adopt herself" (ibid., 253). So, my response to my Catholic friend is not meant to diminish the importance of the "truths" found in the teachings of the Magisterium. Rather, it is to suggest that even the teachings of the Magisterium, as well as the teachings of all other Christian traditions, must be subject to the "higher authority" of the "Truth" that only God fully knows.

2. For various Christian perspectives on postmodernism, see Westphal, *Postmodern Philosophy*; Dockery, *Challenge of Postmodernism*; Greer, *Mapping Postmodernism*; Grenz, *Primer on Postmodernism*; Downing, *Postmodernism Serves (My) Faith*; Haynes, *Postmodern Academy*.

A Future for American Evangelicalism

to reiterating the distinction I made previously between Truth and truth.

A strong version of postmodernism denies the existence of Truth—a position that is antithetical to the Christian faith. But a "soft postmodernism" that I believe comports with the Christian faith is that there is Truth (which God only fully knows), but that as a finite, fallible human being, I only have a partial glimpse (truth) of that Truth that is informed by my particularities, including the particular stream of Evangelicalism is which I am embedded (1 Cor 13:12).

My focus on the priority of Truth comports well with John Hawthorne's assertion that "the search for truth is the central conviction of Christian higher education." Anticipating a later subtopic in this chapter, Hawthorne notes the "danger of prioritizing the protection of a particular position over the search for Truth."

Therefore, the Truth that holds ultimate authority for me is not to be equated with my partial glimpse or the partial glimpses of any other evangelical or stream of Evangelicalism. Rather, it is God's Truth, and I am called to seek better understanding of that Truth in conversation with other evangelicals.

In that light, it saddens me to report that during my forty years of serving fulltime at four different Christian colleges as both a teacher and administrator, I have encountered too many faculty members whose philosophy of Christian higher education effectively amounts to "My particular Christian tradition has captured the full scope of God's Truth, so listen up," or worse yet, "I have the Truth and you don't, so listen up!"

My differing philosophy of Christian higher education, which, I am pleased to report, I share with many other faculty members at Christian colleges, is that Christian higher education, at its best, is a *conversation toward Truth*, and that "safe spaces" need to be provided where conversation partners can express their beliefs with deep conviction while remaining open to listening to the contrary views of others and respectfully talking about their disagreements, with the goal of gaining better mutual understanding of Truth.

Evangelicalism and Higher Education

This philosophy of Christian higher education calls for the type of humility pointed to by Sarah Ruden: "I'm just a person, but God is God; so it doesn't shatter me to admit when I'm wrong or need help." In a similar vein, one of our readers, Bruce P., bemoans "a lack of humility, a lack of ability to be wrong, and from there, a lack of ability to learn. And thus, a lack of ability to grow" that has a detrimental effect on a "genuine pursuit of truth."

My organization of the remainder of this chapter is based on my belief that Christian higher education should be characterized by conversation toward Truth.[3]

CONVERSATION TOWARD TRUTH IS COMMUNAL

Unless you are inclined to talk to yourself, my title for this subsection should go without saying. But, as will soon become apparent, this needs to be said to overcome the strong tendencies toward unencumbered individualism in American culture.

John Hawthorne expresses this communal ideal as we seek better understanding of Truth most succinctly when he holds out the hope for evangelicals that "we can be the Body of Christ in the world coming alongside others in the search for truth."

Recall Ard Louis' suggestion that many of the issues that evangelicals are struggling with (e.g., origins) are so complicated that "no person is smart enough to solve all those things for the church. It has to be a communal thing." Recall also John Franke's assertion that "the diversity of biblical, theological, and confessional perspectives in Evangelicalism and the broader Christian tradition are a necessary and appropriate manifestation of the church. *This is because no single linguistic context or interpretive*

---

3. My view of Christian higher education as a conversation toward Truth comports well with Paul Knitter's more comprehensive observation that such conversation is emerging as the "new way of being Church." He comments, "Dialogue is becoming a meaningful challenging 'new way of being Church,'" going on to describe "dialogue" as "a relationship among differing parties in which all parties both speak their minds and open their minds to each other, in the hope that through this engagement all parties will grow in truth and well-being" (Knitter, "New Way," 95–97).

community is able to bear fully adequate witness to the truth of the living God."[4]

If Franke is correct, as I believe he is, that "no single linguistic context or interpretive community is able to bear adequate witness to the truth of the living God," this raises the crucial question as to how the various evangelical interpretive communities can best work together in a way that will enable each community to make an important contribution to the communal evangelical quest to gain a better understanding of God's Truth. Although our eCircle contributors do not directly address this question, I will now present my dream for such communal collaboration.

TALKING WITHIN AN INSTITUTION AND THEN MOVING OUTWARD

Conversations within and across Evangelical Institutions of Higher Education

The conversation toward Truth first needs to take place within each evangelical institution of Christian higher education. For those evangelical institutions having a particular denominational affiliation, such internal conversations need to be informed by the core theological commitments of that particular stream of Evangelicalism.

For example, the conversations at Calvin College should be deeply informed by various strands of Calvinist theology, the conversations at Goshen College should be deeply informed by Anabaptist theologies, and conversations at Point Loma Nazarene University should be deeply informed by Nazarene theologies. This includes the faculty at such institutions pursuing scholarship that is informed by these particular core theological commitments.

And, if there is any validity to my suggestion that the common ground in the midst of the great diversity of evangelical beliefs consists of adherence to some version of David Bebbington's defining characteristics of biblicism, conversionism, activism, and

---

4. Italics mine.

crucicentrism—however these characteristics may be articulated within the given theological tradition—the conversations at any institution that considers itself to be evangelical needs to also be informed by that institution's particular understanding of these characteristics.

At first glance, one would think that nondenominational evangelical Christian institutions of higher education would be ideal venues for conversation toward Truth, because they have already assembled a diverse group of faculty who represent various streams of Evangelicalism. But that was not my experience while serving at two nondenominational Christian colleges. I found that faculty members representing different theological traditions seldom talked to each other about their theological differences and how these differences might inform their respective understandings of important contemporary issues. Why was that?

For starters, everyone was too busy with the multiple, often onerous responsibilities of being faculty members at a Christian college to take the time needed for such cross-tradition conversations. Secondly, the tendency for faculty members to stay within their "disciplinary silos" militated against such conversations about contemporary issues that begged for interdisciplinary conversation.

But my dream for evangelical conversations toward Truth calls for far more than internal conversations within various evangelical institutions. If I am correct that no particular stream of Evangelicalism has captured all of God's Truth, but each stream has an important contribution to make toward a comprehensive understanding of God's Truth, then conversation toward Truth needs to also take place across evangelical institutions.

For faculty, this means that there must be conversations about the best results of scholarship that take place across evangelical theological traditions and are informed by each tradition, thereby opening up the possibility of scholars from each tradition learning from one another, even to the point of refining or correcting their views on the issues at hand in light of the best insights of other evangelical theological traditions.

A Future for American Evangelicalism

Conversations beyond Evangelical Institutions of Higher Education

But evangelical Christians can also learn from conversations with adherents to other Christian traditions that would not be considered evangelical. Therefore, the conversations that evangelicals have in the quest for Truth need to be expanded to include engagement with non-evangelical Christians

Finally, the circles of conversation need to be expanded to include engagement with non-Christians for two reasons. In light of Christian teachings about "common grace," there are those committed to other faiths, religious or secular, who have important insights that can help evangelicals to better understand their Christian faith and even refine that understanding.

Secondly, I strongly believe that one aspect of the calling that all Christians, but especially Christian scholars, have, is to share our partial glimpses of God's Truth with those committed to other faiths as one means of being agents for God's redemptive purposes for creation.[5] Although our contributors do not address this issue in depth, Kurt Anders Richardson does point to the need for evangelicals to "do public theology," thereby avoiding the kind of "separatism" that will "needlessly marginalize" evangelicals.

This dream of mine for numerous venues for communal conversations toward Truth is surely grandiose, especially considering some major obstacles, a topic to which I now turn (limiting myself here to obstacles within and across evangelical institutions of higher education that are pointed to by our contributors).[6]

---

5. See Heie, "Dialogic Discourse," 347–56, and ibid., *Learning to Listen*, 80–94, 103–13.

6. See ibid., for a consideration of some obstacles when engaging with non-Christians.

Evangelicalism and Higher Education

OBSTACLES TO CONVERSATION TOWARD TRUTH AT EVANGELICAL INSTITUTIONS OF HIGHER EDUCATION

I have already quoted a few of our contributors who suggest that a major obstacle to orchestrating communal conversations toward Truth is the individualism that militates against communal efforts. Other contributors express the same concern.

Justin Barnard expresses this concern strongly when he calls into question "radically individualized plurality," suggesting that "communal narrative unity" should be sought instead.

Barnard points us to a source of such radical individualism when he bemoans the "supremacy of the solitary appetitive Self as the moral center of the universe," wherein "what matters (indeed all that matters) is what I want," suggesting that this individualized focus is reinforced by "the omnipresence of digital technology and the triumph of global consumerism."

Barnard goes on to suggest that "sadly, Christian institutions are, at times, guilty of peddling the lie [that "you will be like gods"]—programmatically and technologically reinforcing the idea that higher education is all about what the student-*qua*-consumer wants." Since "the appetitive soul is insatiable," Barnard explains, "too often (and often too quickly) Christian colleges and universities have unreflectively followed suit: more bandwidth, more courses, more majors, more programs, more facilities."

Barnard dares to conclude that "the challenge for Christian higher education in the twenty-first century is to learn that less is more. Meaning must take precedence over quantity. Formation should be favored over mere information," and as I have already quoted, "communal narrative unity" must take precedence over "radically individualized plurality."

In a response to Barnard's posting, Nicholas Rowe, who teaches in South Africa, asserts that the obstacle Barnard points to is not limited to higher education in America, noting his experience that "for students there is absolutely no place for reflection at all. They are not being formed; they are not being educated, but

A Future for American Evangelicalism

are being 'trained' for the purposes of the economy and the state." Of course, a savvy Christian college or university administrator will be quick to point out, quite legitimately, that if we don't pay attention to what prospective students want, we will soon be out of business. But no one is saying that we should pay no attention to what students want, especially relative to preparation for a career. As is often the case relative to thorny tensions, it is a matter of discerning the best balance, in two ways.

First, even specialized education in preparation for a career can incorporate conversations toward Truth by going beyond training in narrowly defined vocational skills to include conversations about the foundational philosophical assumptions that underlie every academic discipline in an attempt to uncover connections between academic knowledge and biblical and theological understanding.[7]

Along these lines, Jim Skillen, in a response to the posting from Amos Yong, points to the need for students preparing for particular jobs to be critical of the "current demands and behavior patterns of institutions in the job market." Skillen explains:

> Even at a Christian colleges students may expect that the Christian faith belongs in worship services, Bible studies, and perhaps some evangelization off campus, while academic work is taken to be intellectual preparation for jobs or further study that takes for granted the current demands and behavior patterns of institutions in the job market.

Skillen expands his concern about the lack of critical engagement relative to the nature of the jobs that students are preparing for to a concern about the lack of communal critical engagement with all that students are learning and all that is being taught. He writes, "the actual work of Christian critical engagement with what we are learning and teaching may be relatively weak, largely individual, and not sufficiently communal."

---

7. Ibid., "Christian Perspective," 95–116.

Evangelicalism and Higher Education

A second area where Christian colleges and universities need to create a better balance between what students want and initiations into broader conversations toward Truth relates to co-curricular activities. In my estimation, too many co-curricular offerings at Christian colleges and universities are intended to be "diversions from learning," rather than opportunities for significant learning outside of the classroom setting. A lot more could be done to orchestrate communal conversations toward Truth outside of the classroom by which all members of the academic community talk respectfully about their agreements and disagreements regarding important contemporary issues.[8]

While touching on the nature of co-curricular activities at evangelical institutions of higher education, it is important to note Amos Yong's exhortation that Christian education at its best cannot be thought of solely in "intellectual terms." Instead, it must address the need for synergy between "the head, the heart, and the hands" wrought by the "renewing and transforming work of the Holy Spirit." Yong explains:

---

8. This strategy of orchestrating communal conversations toward Truth outside of the college classroom has been marvelously exemplified by means of an annual Gordon College Symposium that has been offered since 1998. A week is devoted to this symposium during each spring semester at Gordon, including evening programming all week and one full day for which all classes are cancelled. An interdisciplinary symposium theme is announced each fall (e.g., "Who Is My Neighbor?" or "The Coming of Global Christianity," and "Money and Possessions"). Students are then given the opportunity to design symposium sessions pertinent to the theme. These have included lecture-type presentations (with students at the lectern and some faculty sitting in the student chairs), poetry readings, a panel of students from a class dealing with an interdisciplinary issue related to the course material, musical compositions, art exhibits, and other venues as varied as the imaginations of students (including a pig roast on the quad one year). This annual event has featured as many as seventy student-initiated projects over the one-week period, with conversations about the materials presented expected as part of each design. Total student attendance for the week has exceeded three thousand, exceptional for a student body of about fifteen hundred. This has been a co-curricular vehicle for students to take more responsibility for their own learning and for making students, co-curricular staff, and faculty equal co-participants in "conversations toward Truth."

A Future for American Evangelicalism

Pedagogically, without denying that education in the modern world has taken form in primarily intellectual terms, there is a growing realization that there are moral, affective, embodied, social/communal, and spiritual dimensions of learning that are no less intrinsic to the formation of whole and holy persons in the service of Christ... [T]his is not to undermine higher education as the pursuit of the life of the mind; it is to emphasize that the intellectual life is reducible to the cognitive register to our peril. Knowledge is not merely a matter of the head but also of hearts (whole persons) and hands (the pragmatic or, in evangelical terms, missional aspect).

I propose the bold suggestion that renewalists ought to be at the forefront of thinking through how this alignment of head-heart-hands enables formation of learners able to bridge academy-church-world for the glory of God. What this means is that the historic evangelical mantras of being biblically-based and Christ-centered are incomplete in as much as that the renewing and transforming work of the Holy Spirit remains neglected. If expanded in this direction, evangelical and renewal higher education is biblically-based, Christ-centered, and Spirit-filled/inspired/empowered.

This exhortation comports well with the biblical teaching that Truth cannot be equated solely with the cognitive dimension of personhood, as pointed to in the biblical reference to "the truth of your life."[9]

The obstacles to conversations toward Truth at evangelical institutions of higher education that our contributors point to above mostly deal with teaching pedagogy and programming (curricular or co-curricular) at such institutions. I will add a more subtle and, in my estimation, more insidious "attitudinal" obstacle to conversations toward Truth: the prideful assumption that we have already captured the complete Truth about the issue at hand, which evidences itself in a failure to acknowledge that *we may be wrong*.

---

9. 3 John 1:3. As pointed out by Marv Wilson, this broad view of the meaning of "truth" comports with the "Hebrew View of Knowledge": "For the Hebrew, to 'know' was to 'do.'" (Wilson, *Father Abraham*, 288).

Evangelicalism and Higher Education

John Howard Yoder points us to our need to acknowledge that we may be wrong:

> The certainty in which we have to act one day at a time must never claim *finality*. Our recognition that we may be wrong must always be *visible*. One way to say this would be to begin every statement one ever makes with "as far as I know" or "until further notice." That I do not begin every paragraph this way does not mean that I do not mean it.[10]

Peter C. Blum relates this insight from Yoder to his call for "patience" in public discourse: "This patience amounts to more than simply a polite fallibilist admission that the probability of my being wrong never reaches zero. Yoder spells it out precisely in terms of the need for one's fallibility to be embodied in discourse."[11]

Yoder has much to teach us here.[12] I must express my dismay at how rare it is for me to hear someone say, "I may be wrong."[13]

10. Yoder, "'Patience' as Method," 31.

11. Blum, "Yoder's Patience," 116. See also n. 14. [x-ref]

12. It should be apparent that the aspects of the work of John Howard Yoder to which I have made reference comport well with my overarching commitment to respectful conversation with those who disagree with me, which is informed by attitudes of humility, patience, courage, and love. But the tension remains between my willingness to embrace Yoder's approach to engagement with others and my rejection of Yoder's suggestion (see n. 4, P. 70) that Christians should eschew the broken world of government-sponsored politics in favor of an "alternative politics" that focuses on modeling an alternative way of life in our Christian communities. My final reflection on this tension is based on Yoder's rejection of "looking for the right 'handle' by which one can 'get a hold on' the course of history and move it in the right direction" (Yoder, *Politics of Jesus*, 234). Granting that much of government-sponsored politics involves exercising coercive power at its worst, I do not view my engagement in the political realm as seeking to "mold the world to my vision" (the "domination" motif in politics that I reject). Rather, I view my engagement in government-sponsored politics as an attempt to sow some "seeds of redemption" through the exercise of the "power of love, humility, patience and courage." So, as I have already said, I think it is a false choice to be expected to choose between seeking to be an agent of redemption in the current broken political system and modeling a redemptive way of life within my Christian community. I believe it should be both-and rather than either-or.

13. I am still waiting to hear those four words on MSNBC or Fox TV News.

To admit such fallibility is to make oneself vulnerable, which we all too often avoid like the plague. Those affiliated with evangelical institutions of higher education must commit themselves to such "dialogical vulnerability" if their institutions are to be welcoming places for conversations toward Truth.

I now turn to what I consider to be another major obstacle at evangelical institutions of higher education to the orchestrating of conversations toward Truth: the tension between the quest for Truth and the particular theological commitments of the institution. I will consider this tension in some detail for two reasons. First, a number of our contributors pointed to this very real tension. Secondly, my perception is that this tension is increasing at an alarming rate at a number of evangelical institutions of higher education, and we need to address it head-on.

Tension between the Quest for Truth and Institutional Core Theological Commitments

The thorny tension that needs to be addressed is posed in one of Rob Barrett's leading questions: "For many, the essence of the university is the pursuit of truth, no matter where it leads. How should evangelical institutions respond when this pursuit appears to come into tension with doctrinal commitments?"

Jeannine Brown notes that the faculty handbook at her own evangelical institution of higher education speaks of the "inevitable tension" that arises "from the pursuit of knowledge with the value of academic freedom and the confessional parameters of an evangelical institution," adding that "this tension is a given in any school that is both confessional and academic."

Brown also notes the fear that scholars can experience as a result of this tension when she asks whether the work of scholars "could bring them into conflict with the confessional stances of an institution in such a way that they would fear bringing their full learning and selves to their scholarship?" Contrast this experience of fear on the part of some Christian scholars with the dream expressed by Karl Giberson: "evangelical higher education needs

Evangelicalism and Higher Education

to loosen up and embrace the truths of its mission statements with the sort of confidence that welcomes dissenting views into the conversation and even onto the faculty."

What is the root cause of this "inevitable tension," and when this tension approaches a breaking point in the scholarly work of any given faculty member, how can it best be navigated?

PROTECTING THE IDENTITY OF AN EVANGELICAL CHRISTIAN INSTITUTION OF HIGHER EDUCATION

To set a proper context for this topic and the subtopics that follow, it is important for me to note the distinction that Robert Benne makes between faith-based institutions of higher education that are Orthodox, Critical-Mass, Intentionally Pluralist, or Accidentally Pluralist.[14] In what immediately follows, I will be considering only institutions that Benne would classify as "orthodox," by which he means schools "requiring that all ongoing members of the academic community subscribe to a statement of belief."[15] Under this definition of "orthodox," all member institutions of the Coalition for Christian Colleges and Universities (CCCU) would be classified as orthodox, since one of the requirements for membership is that the institution "hire only persons who profess faith in Jesus Christ as full-time faculty members and administrators."[16] To stipulate that one must be a Christian to be hired is surely a minimalist statement of belief, but it is a statement of belief nevertheless.

So, our immediate task is to consider what might to be necessary to protect the identity of an orthodox evangelical Christian institution of higher education.

Citing some of the literature on the secularization of Christian institutions of higher education in the past,[17] Rick Ostrander

14. Benne, *Quality with Soul*.
15. Ibid., 50.
16. Council for Christian Colleges and Universities, "Members and Affiliates," *CCU.org*, 2015, http://www.cccu.org/members_and_affiliates.
17. Marsden, *American University*; Burtchaell, *Dying of the Light*.

notes that "this nagging fear of inevitable secularization . . . still pervades the culture of evangelical higher education," so much so that "some evangelicals seemingly view any change as inevitably leading to secularization." Ostrander embraces the possibility for "positive change," but suggests that "we need to balance our ambition for positive change with a sense of humility and caution learned through the lessons of history and the laws of unintended consequences," being "concerned with losing our distinctive Christian identity."

Ostrander then poses the question, "How do we avoid secularization in our quest for positive change and growth?" He provides three responses: "First, we need a clearly-articulated statement of our core beliefs and values," adding that "especially at a non-denominational university such as mine, it's crucial that we do the difficult work of formulating a simple, clear statement of theological convictions which members of the community can understand and affirm, and do so without a wink and a nod."

Secondly, since "it's the board of trustees that sets the vision of the university, and that will sustain the vision, primarily through the hiring of a president," vigilance needs to be exercised as to who sits on the membership committee of the Board of Trustees.

Finally, Ostrander paraphrases Bill Clinton to insist, "It's the faculty, stupid," since "Professors are the heart and soul of a university." In his response to a comment posted by John Hawthorne, Ostrander concludes that "if we put the hard work into hiring well, then we can provide faculty with the academic freedom to delve into difficult issues, and defend their right to do so."

From my many years of experience serving as both a faculty member and Chief Academic Officer at various Christian colleges affiliated with the CCCU, I personally affirm Rick Ostrander's position on orthodox schools summarized above (leaving open for the time being the question of how extensive the school's "statement of core beliefs and values" should be).

But, from my experience when asked to consult at a few CCCU colleges where the tension between the quest for Truth and institutional theological commitments had reached a breaking

Evangelicalism and Higher Education

point, it is important for me to point out a pernicious potential abuse of the attempt to protect the identity of a Christian institution of higher education, which a number of our contributors also point to.

IMPLICIT CONSTRAINTS ON THE QUEST FOR TRUTH THAT GO BEYOND EXPLICIT THEOLOGICAL COMMITMENTS

Jeannine Brown points to this pernicious potential problem with deep conviction and great clarity when she asserts:

> It is important for evangelical seminaries and universities to come clean about their implicit constraints for hiring and maintaining their faculty. If a confessional stance is communicated in a published statement of faith that is clear upon hiring . . . then there's a chance for faculties to walk the fine line between academic freedom and confessional agreement. *But when informal but real constraints beyond those clearly delineated are at work, the task of credible scholarship becomes more difficult.*[18]

Brown provides an excellent example of her concern from her own experience at an evangelical seminary:

> Bethel Seminary, like many seminaries, has a statement of faith in which we affirm a particular view on the nature of Scripture. Whatever the terminology used (e.g., inspired, infallible, inerrant), evangelical seminaries tend to have an explicit statement about the authority of the biblical text. Yet what often happens in faculty hiring, promotion, tenure, and review goes beyond ensuring that faculty have signed on to the institution's statement of faith. Typically, there are additional and often implicit expectations about specific interpretations that presumably arise from the shared belief in Scripture's authority (and go beyond the rest of the faith statement, which usually addresses core theological beliefs). In this

18. Italics mine.

scenario, assumptions about interpretations arising from an "evangelical hermeneutic" lead to constraints that move beyond the written page of an explicit statement of faith.

At this point, Brown invokes the work of Kevin Vanhoozer in asserting:

> The belief in any particular formation of biblical authority (in his argument, inerrancy) is not yet a set of interpretations. A particular view of biblical authority is an "underdetermined hermeneutic."[19] It does not assure the same interpretive conclusions. To assume that the one inevitably leads to the other (e.g., that a high view of Scripture necessitates certain, particular conclusions) is to confuse issues of authority and hermeneutics.

Vanhoozer's call for Christians to not "confuse issues of authority and hermeneutics" is particularly relevant to a recurring theme in this book: Evangelicals who hold equally to the authority of the Bible can nevertheless interpret the same passage of Scripture differently when they engage in the task of doing biblical hermeneutics, often reflecting their particular social locations, including the particular streams of Evangelicalism within which they are embedded.

Karl Giberson tells of his painful experience while teaching in a Church of the Nazarene college where the explicit stance of his denomination "rejected biblical literalism," but where there was nevertheless an implicit hostility at the "grassroots" level to his teaching that God created though evolutionary means, apparently because it ran counter to "biblical literalism." As Giberson explains, "Although the Church of the Nazarene explicitly rejected biblical literalism and its scholars were almost unanimous in endorsing evolution, the grassroots hostility to evolution was overwhelming—and leadership was simply unwilling to stand up for science." This perceived lack of institutional courage will be discussed in further detail later.

---

19. Vanhoozer, "Lost in Interpretation," 97.

Evangelicalism and Higher Education

I have my own story to tell about a CCCU university where an "implicit" constraint on the quest for Truth trumped the university's more open explicit constraint, as I indicated online in my response to Jeannine Brown's posting.[20]

Trouble was brewing at this particular CCCU university because certain faculty were allowing for the possibility that God created through evolutionary means. I was invited to speak to the faculty, presumably because I might be able to calm some troubled waters.[21] As has always been my practice when asked to speak or consult at a college or university, I went online to carefully read the statement of core doctrinal commitments of this university (since I like to hold institutions to their own words about what they consider to be important). What I found surprised me.

The core doctrinal beliefs of this university clearly asserted *that* God created the universe. But not a word was said about *how* God created the universe. So, for whatever reason, an implicit constraint that precluded God creating through evolutionary means was trumping the university's explicit statement of doctrinal beliefs. I shared with the faculty words to the effect that "this silence in [the university's] foundational beliefs about 'how' God created provides a legitimate 'safe space' for hiring [and keeping] faculty who disagree about this issue, and the institution should provide venues where those who disagree can have respectful conversation about their disagreements toward the goal of adequately understanding the nature of their differences and ultimately learning from one another." I added words to the effect that "it was unfortunate that 'informal but real constraints beyond those clearly delineated' truncated the possibility of faculty pursuing further research about this important issue and talking to each other, and their students, about the results of their research."

---

20. In my role as co-moderator for this eCircle, I seldom submitted comments. But in this case, given some of my own hard-earned experience, I couldn't resist.

21. After publication of my *Learning to Listen* in 2007, I was invited to speak at a number of CCCU institutions that were experiencing significant conflict over doctrinal disagreements.

A Future for American Evangelicalism

WHY ARE THERE IMPLICIT CONSTRAINTS ON THE QUEST FOR TRUTH?

Meddlesome as I can be at times, while always aspiring to be respectful, I responded to Jeannine Brown's posting with a piece I entitled "The Elephant in the Room," in which I posed the question as to why some Christian institutions of higher education impose informal but real constraints on the quest for Truth beyond those clearly delineated in their doctrinal statements.

I responded to my own question with one answer that I have heard spoken or seen implied too many times in my forty years of service at four Christian liberal arts colleges:

> Even if disagreement about this particular controversial issue is not precluded by our school's statement or beliefs, what will our constituents think (or do) if they knew that we allowed faculty and students to disagree about this particular issue and openly talk about our disagreements in campus venues? Will some of our constituents stop sending us our students and their money?

I further suggested that "such a response reflects a huge lack of the Christian virtues of 'courage' and 'faith' at the institutional level," and suggested the contours of what I would consider to be a courageous response to a disgruntled constituent:

> If confronted by a constituent who is unhappy about the college or seminary allowing disagreements and open conversation about a given issue concerning which the institution has not taken a stance (in its statement of beliefs), and about which that constituent may firmly believe that she has "the Christian answer," a Christian college or seminary administrator ought to have the courage to say something like: "We intend to remain steadfastly true to our institution's statement of beliefs, but as an educational institution we also intend to remain steadfastly true to our educational philosophy, which encourages faculty research and campus-wide conversation about issues for which our statement of beliefs allows room for equally committed Christians to disagree."

Evangelicalism and Higher Education

That response is actually a summary of what I once said to a very disgruntled parent of one of our students in my former life as a Chief Academic Officer at a Christian college—I don't think I changed his mind, but he needed to hear these words from me as a representative of the college. I don't know if that parent stopped supporting the college, either through the continuing enrollment of his son or with his money. But what if he did stop his support? Here is my response:

> To those who worry about a Christian college or seminary losing constituents and supporters because of an insistence on remaining true to its core theological and educational beliefs, I dare to ask the question: "Cannot God raise up new constituents who will support us precisely because we remained true to our core theological beliefs and to an unyielding commitment to seek after Truth as only God fully understands it?"

I was not deluged with contributor responses to my *why* question. But John Hawthorne did respond by suggesting that "the fact that we've often been caught up in much more 'worldly' values of prestige and access to donors [than to the "pursuit of Truth"] is . . . troubling," adding that "it is a courageous institution that simultaneously celebrates deep faith in God and a willingness to explore Truth through whatever paths necessary. It's a model of education the broader society desperately needs."

WHAT SORT OF EXPLICIT DOCTRINAL COMMITMENTS SHOULD EVANGELICAL INSTITUTIONS OF HIGHER EDUCATION HAVE?

This was one of the leading questions posed by Rob Barrett. As you can no doubt tell from the above long and rather passionate narrative, I am dismayed at the way turmoil can be generated at evangelical institutions of higher education when implicit constraints on the quest for Truth trump the institution's public statement of core theological beliefs, often reflecting a lack of courage and faith on the part of the institutional leadership.

But this abuse does not nullify the need pointed out by Rick Ostrander for each orthodox evangelical institution for higher education to have a "clearly articulated statement of core beliefs and values." But what type of statement should that be, and how detailed, or not, should it be? Our contributors did not address this question directly, so I will take a stab at a response.

It is obvious that a particular orthodox evangelical denomination that sponsors and supports an educational institution is free to define the statement of core beliefs and values that should govern that institution. But my advice in such a case would be to develop a minimalist statement that is limited to those core beliefs that are deemed to be absolutely essential to maintaining the integrity of the denomination's Christian tradition, thereby allowing room for conversations toward Truth about issues were there is disagreement within the denomination.

For nondenominational evangelical institutions of higher education, I would again recommend a minimalist statement. With respect to core theological beliefs, I would orchestrate a community-wide conversation, starting with consideration of David Bebbington's four defining characteristics of Evangelicalism, with the goal of articulating a consensus understanding of the meaning of these characteristics, or some variation thereof, that would then comprise the institution's core theological beliefs—no more and no less.

As an aside (since this is a book on American Evangelicalism not American Christianity), if I were asked to articulate the core theological beliefs for a new *Christian* university, I would propose the following minimalist statement: *We are committed to be followers of Jesus aspiring to live in faithful obedience to the two great commandments of Jesus to love God with all our hearts, souls, and minds, and to love our neighbors as ourselves.* If you think this statement of theological belief is too minimalist, I remind you that it appears to be sufficient for the CCCU that faculty members profess to be Christian.

Evangelicalism and Higher Education

WHAT SHOULD BE DONE WHEN THE TENSION BETWEEN A FACULTY MEMBER'S QUEST FOR TRUTH AND THE INSTITUTION'S CORE DOCTRINAL COMMITMENTS APPEARS TO BE IRRECONCILABLE?

However extensive or minimalist an institution's core theological beliefs are, a point can be reached where the tension between a faculty member's quest for Truth and these core beliefs appears to be irreconcilable. How should the faculty member and the institution then proceed?

I start with how I would proceed as a faculty member. I have signed many statements of core beliefs and practices at Christian colleges, but never with a wink and a nod.[22] If in my quest for Truth, I ever reached a point where I could no longer affirm a core belief or agree to live by a core practice of a Christian college where I was employed, the priority I give to maintaining my personal integrity would require that I resign my faculty appointment and continue my quest for Truth elsewhere. In other words, for me, the pursuit of Truth is far more important than any job or institutional affiliation. So, if I find my quest for Truth compromised by the explicit commitments of the institution I am serving, then my commitment to continue on that quest for Truth, come what may, demands that I continue that quest elsewhere.

Given that personal conviction on my part, how would I proceed if, in my role as a Chief Academic Officer at a CCCU college, I had good reason to believe that one of my faculty members could no longer affirm the college's core beliefs and practices? As you might guess by now, I would have a conversation with that faculty member.[23]

---

22. For example, in my first teaching position at the King's College in New York from 1963 to 1975, I annually signed a "Pledge" that included the stipulation that I would not attend movies. Although I found no biblical basis for such a prohibition, I kept my word for the sake of my integrity and my teaching ministry at that school.

23. I am thankful that I never had to have the type of conversation that I describe here during my thirteen years as a Chief Academic Officer at two

A Future for American Evangelicalism

Although, as I like to say, you cannot predict beforehand the results of a genuine conversation, the questions I would pose to the faculty member in this hypothetical case would include the following.

- Where has your quest for Truth led you?
- What is your perception of the relationship between the results of your quest for Truth and the institution's statement of beliefs that you had once affirmed?
- If you can no longer affirm the institution's statement of beliefs, what course of action do you think will be best for both your ongoing growth and for the institution?
- If you were to remain as a faculty member, in what ways do you think you can contribute to accomplishing the educational mission of the institution?

This hypothetical conversation could lead the faculty member to conclude that resignation from the institution is the best course of action. But if the conversation reveals a compelling case for continuing employment, and if the conversation led me to believe that this faculty member's commitment to seek the Truth served both him or her and the institution well, I would take the position that his or her employment should be continued. My primary reason for this conclusion is my unwillingness to disenfranchise a faculty member who is deeply committed to the search for Truth and whose ongoing quest for Truth has the potential to foster his or her growth and also reap significant benefits for the institution and its students.

Of course, this hypothetical conversation may not go that well. If it were instead to lead to the conclusion that continuing employment would have a severe detrimental effect on the very core of the institution and, at least in the long run, on the faculty member, then I would initiate termination of employment

---

Christian colleges. Ironically, the only conversation I had that was in the neighborhood of what I describe here was when a faculty member expressed concern that his expression of Christian faith did not fit the college's statement of beliefs and I pointed out to him that this was not the case.

procedures, using all the elements of due process stipulated in the faculty handbook and taking great care to do all that I could for the faculty member during a difficult time of transition.

But wouldn't continuing the employment of such a faculty member amount to a double standard? Most faculty need to affirm the statement of beliefs in its entirety; others can get away with denying a stipulation or two. My initial response is that if I were the Chief Academic Officer at any orthodox Christian college or university, I would extend the same courtesy of this type of conversation to any faculty member, and this courtesy would be stipulated in the faculty handbook (leaving open the question as to whether the president and board would allow for such an approach on the part of the Chief Academic Officer—if not, I would need to struggle with the question of whether I could, with integrity, continue in my position).

However, I conclude this section with an even more radical proposal. Up to this point I have been talking about an attempt to navigate the tension between a faculty member's quest for Truth and an institution's theological commitments for those faith-based institutions that Benne classifies as "orthodox." After a career of serving at orthodox institutions (for which I have no regrets), I have come to the hard-earned conclusion that the "conversation toward Truth" ideal that I embrace has greater potential for realization at faith-based institutions that Benne classifies as "Critical-Mass."

Benne defines Critical-Mass colleges and universities as follows: "[They] do not insist that all members of the community be believers in their tradition or even believers in the Christian tradition, though they do insist that a critical mass of adherents from their tradition inhabit all the constituencies of the educational enterprise—board, administration, faculty and student body," adding that it is up to each institution to define a "critical mass." In brief, the stipulation that a critical-mass of these various constituencies must adhere to the core Christian beliefs of the institution will serve to protect the identity of the Christian institution (however challenging that may be at times) while opening up the communal conversation to a significant number of dissenting voices, which will enhance the quest for Truth.

WHAT SHOULD BE DONE WHEN THE INSTITUTION'S CORE COMMITMENTS ARE CALLED INTO QUESTION?

In the previous subsection, I addressed the difficult issue of how to proceed when a faculty member's quest for Truth and the institution's core doctrinal commitments appear to be in irreconcilable conflict. As challenging as that can be, an even more difficult situation is when a particular core commitment of the institution in terms of doctrinal or behavioral issues is called into question by a number of faculty or staff and constituents. At some critical level of dissatisfaction that it impossible to define exactly, the institution's board of trustees, which bears primary responsibility for the wellbeing of the institution, may conclude that careful study and consideration must be given to the question of whether a particular core commitment needs to be reframed or even dropped.

Lest you think this is strictly a theoretical question, there are at least two CCCU schools that have recently entered into what they have called a period of "discernment" to consider questions regarding institutional stances on issues related to homosexuality, such as whether or not to hire faculty who identify as members of the LGBTQ community or behavioral expectations for students, faculty, and staff.

It is obviously up to each such institution to define the contours of a discernment process (for this issue or any other thorny problems the institution may be grappling with). Therefore, I will limit myself to a few reflections that flow from the content of this chapter and the major themes of this book.

The ideal, for me, is that this discernment process create safe spaces that welcome a plethora of alternative views as to whether the current core commitment should be reframed or dropped, with open and respectful conversation about the merits, or otherwise, of these alternative views and with no negative consequences for those who propose reframing or dropping the core commitment. But this ideal may be difficult to attain at what Benne classifies as "orthodox" Christian institutions of higher education (like all CCCU schools) where, to continue their employment, all faculty and staff are expected to affirm and abide by an institutional statement of behavioral expectations and beliefs.

The problem, as I see it, at orthodox institutions is not with agreed-upon behavioral expectations, since faculty or staff members are generally free to disagree with a particular behavioral expectation as long as they behave in accordance with the expectation. Rather, the problem is with expectations relative to "theological beliefs," since faculty or staff members have affirmed their agreement with stipulated theological beliefs, and to renege on that affirmation subjects faculty or staff members to the possibility of termination of employment (or, at a minimum, to the process I outlined in the previous section).

Therefore, it seems to me that it is not realistic to think that an orthodox institution can create a safe space that welcomes a variety of alternative views regarding a current core theological belief—a space in which it can be assured that there will be no negative consequences for those who, by articulating a need to drop or modify that belief, are indicating their disagreement with the belief.

If we grant that it may sometimes be appropriate to change an existing theological belief at an orthodox institution, the question looms as to how that may be possible. It appears to me that it will require that a significant number of faculty or staff articulate the need for change despite the potential for negative consequences for them should the final result of the discernment process affirm the theological belief as-is. Is that a realistic expectation?

My perception that the ideal for a discernment process such as I note above is difficult to attain at an orthodox institution further reinforces the conclusion I have reached (after serving my entire career at orthodox institutions) that the "conversation toward Truth" ideal that I embrace for Christian higher education has greater potential for realization at Christian institutions of higher education that fall into Benne's category of "Critical Mass" institutions, where not all faculty and staff have to agree with an institutional statement of core beliefs as long as a "critical mass" affirm those core beliefs.

SPECIAL WORDS OF ADVICE FOR EVANGELICAL SEMINARIES

Although most of the postings of our contributors applied most directly to evangelical colleges and universities, a few of our contributors offered some concrete advice to evangelical seminaries in their postings on previous topics.

In the conversation on "Evangelicalism and Morality," Vincent Bacote suggested that "in the ongoing discussions of the future of seminaries, perhaps one area of improvement could be to better integrate ethics into classes that mainly focus on exegetical and doctrinal concerns."

In the conversation on "Evangelicalism and Scientific Models of Humanity and Cosmic and Human Origins," Kyle Roberts suggests that seminaries need to allow science "to have a prominently descriptive role" in the study of evangelical theology.

In the chapter on "Evangelicalism and the Modern Study of Scripture," Christopher Hays bemoans the fact that "our best and brightest [students of theology] have not engaged historical criticism with the same vigor that they've applied to exegesis, linguistics, and doctrine," which has clear implications for teaching and learning at evangelical seminaries.

9

The Future of American Evangelicalism

A COMPREHENSIVE GOSPEL OF RECONCILIATION

John Hawthorne perceives the mood of the "younger generation" of evangelicals as having "increased concern for those who are powerless (the poor, the trafficked, the innocent)" that "prioritizes compassion over being right and separate." In my estimation, this focus on addressing the needs of those Jesus called "the least of these" (Matt 25:40, 45) points to the possibility of a vibrant future for Evangelicalism.

Kyle Roberts elaborates by pointing us toward a broad view of "God's reconciliation with the world" that includes but goes beyond the "reconciliation of people with God" to also include the reconciliation of people with each other and with all of God's creation. Roberts writes:

> I cannot state strongly enough that to be an *evangelical* Christian ought to signify, above anything else, a commitment to the gospel. But this raises the debated

A Future for American Evangelicalism

question as to what exactly the gospel is. The future of evangelical Christianity—its health, vibrancy, and relevance for the world—depends on the articulation of the full-bodied, holistic gospel of Jesus Christ. That gospel is the unparalleled story of *God's project of reconciliation*. It is the good news of God entering the world in Jesus and the Spirit and bringing creation from brokenness toward its ultimate healing, wholeness and purpose. This reconciliation is of people with God, but also of people with each other, people with themselves (the healing toward wholeness and holiness of fractured, broken people), and people with God's creation.[1]

As he goes on to add, Roberts envisions a "future of evangelical Christianity . . . that embraces both the vertical dimension of salvation (justification and reconciliation with God) and the horizontal dimension of salvation (healing, relational wholeness and peace, liberation from oppression)." Roberts adds that "his gospel of reconciliation does not depend on the power and strength of institutional Christianity and speaks a prophetic word against the conflation of political power and the Christian religion (what Kierkegaard, among others, called *Christendom*)."

Jeannine Brown strikes a similar note in calling our attention to the healthy "activism" of the current generation of students she teaches at her seminary who are committed to "living out the gospel." She writes, "They are activists who care about human suffering and who desire deeply to live out the gospel—the story of Jesus—in their particular communities, empowered by the Spirit, for God's honor, and for the world's restoration." She adds that they are committed to "living out justice, mercy, and faithfulness."

As has been addressed earlier in this book, we also need to be constantly reminded that this "holistic gospel of Jesus Christ" needs to be addressed to "whole persons," informing the cognitive, affective, and volitional dimensions of personhood. We are not disembodied intellects (what others have called "brains on a stick"). The good news of the gospel should inform not only what

---

1. Italics mine.

The Future of American Evangelicalism

we believe, but also our affections and how we live out what we say we believe (the proverbial wedding of the head, heart, and hands).

UNITY IN THE MIDST OF DIVERSITY

In the introductory chapter, I seconded John Franke's view that the diversity within Evangelicalism should be embraced as "the blessing and intention of God." In the electronic conversation that informs this chapter, Jeannine Brown echoes this sentiment, saying that "I . . . hope . . . we might celebrate the breadth and diversity that is American Evangelicalism," noting with approval Amos Yong's concern that "we intentionally include non-white populations in our conceptions of Evangelicalism," and asking the questions, "How do we do justice to the presence of immigrant movements within American Evangelicalism? How will be pay attention to and learn from global evangelical expressions?"

But is there any hope for unity in the midst of this marvelous diversity? Amy Black says that her "hope is that American evangelicals can unite in ways that allow us to become a force for positive change" for transforming society and culture. But what can unite evangelicals to be such a positive force?

John Wilson says that we need to focus on the "great truths that unite us." More specifically, John Hawthorne paraphrases Ken Schenck's argument that "there is great value in focusing on the broad common themes of the scriptural story rather than on the verses that divide."[2] But what are these "great truths" and common scriptural themes that can serve to unite us?

This entire manuscript has been leading up to my proposal that Kyle Roberts' reference to "God's project of reconciliation" may be the "Center" that can hold evangelicals together in the midst of our great diversity in belief and ecclesiastical practice. We are all called to be agents for God's redemptive purposes, partnering with God in the task of reconciliation in all areas of life to sow

2. Schenck, "Common Denominator."

seeds of redemption that provide glimpses of the fully realized kingdom of God to come (Matt 13:31–32).

In that light, I will reiterate, for emphasis, the synergy I perceive between my articulations of Bebbington's four characteristics of Evangelicalism around the integrative thread of "God's project of reconciliation": Crucicentrism holds that God's project of reconciliation, made possible through the life, death, and resurrection of Jesus Christ, extends to all areas of life. Activism holds that Christians are called to partner with God in God's project of reconciliation. Conversionism points to the commitment to be a follower of Jesus that is to be the primary motivation for seeking to partner with God in God's project of reconciliation. And biblicism points us to the authority of the Bible as the primary source of teachings on how to understand our faith commitment and to put our profession of Christian faith into practice as we partner with God in God's project of reconciliation.

COLLABORATING ACROSS TRADITIONS

Recalling John Hawthorne's perception that younger evangelicals eschew "separatism," Jeannine Brown notes her seminary students' desire to "collaborate and be in conversation with those not just like them, theologically or socially." She explains:

> What particularly excites me about the work of this next generation is their willingness to collaborate and to be in conversation with those not just like them, theologically or socially. There is a sense of the importance of relationality in their work and presence that I find exceedingly hopeful. Capable hands, it seems to me, for a passing of the torch, even and especially if this next generation doesn't do Evangelicalism precisely like each past generation has envisioned it.

Similarly, Amy Black encourages evangelicals to take advantage of the many "opportunities for multiethnic and multiracial collaborations." On a stronger note, Sarah Ruden asserts that there is not a promising future for American Evangelicalism if we do not

The Future of American Evangelicalism

rethink our "Americanness" and build solidarity with Christians worldwide:

> I don't think American Evangelicalism has any meaningful future if it keeps classing itself as "American," a sort of separate national religion. As a distinct movement and culture in the United States, it can only lampoon its own professed theology and wall itself off from the aspirations, sufferings, and perils of Christianity worldwide.
>
> The differences in the American Christian experience—not only in Evangelicalism, but pretty much across the board—make it hard for believers to understand how far we are from the early church that was born along with basic Christian ideas, whereas many Latin American, African, and Asian congregations do have that closer view. Unless we can imagine a future along with them, we might as well chuck it in, in my opinion.
>
> I like to call myself a Christian, but because American is a stronger part of my identity, I have bought my faith very cheaply—if in my circumstances it can be called faith at all. Alas, in recent years, with more Americans losing their homes, going hungry, and dying from lack of the medical care than even a comfortable fellow citizen can ignore, I'm being forced into a greater sense of Christian realities even here; but that means having to rethink my deepest Americanness, the belief that my country must be a special, protected, privileged part of God's plan.
>
> American culture and American power, in short, pretty systematically exclude us from the kind of solidarity with Christians and potential Christians worldwide that would give our faith a truly solidified and revitalized future. If we are to have this, our allegiances need a serious revamp.

A Future for American Evangelicalism

FROM COMBATIVENESS TO OPENNESS

Drawing on James Davison Hunter's recent book,[3] John Hawthorne expresses his belief that for American Evangelicalism, "the next decade will see an outbreak of Faithful Presence over more combative views of faith and culture," where a defining characteristic of "Faithful Presence," for Hawthorne, is "trying to live as citizens of the kingdom of God."

Hawthorne suggests:

> It's entirely possible that the short term will see more combative language from many quarters . . . If the past four decades of American Evangelicalism has been defined by the power dynamics of culture wars, it's going to be hard for major players (and their intellectual heirs) to simply give up the fight. Over the long run, however, the posturing and argumentation of the former style will prove no match for the honesty and humility of Faithful Presence. This is because the Defensive Against posture must rely on overstatement, generalization, and politicization while Faithful Presence depends on old-fashioned testimony. To tell one's story of faith in the midst of complexity yields an authenticity that is beyond reproach.

It can be argued that the combativeness of Evangelicalism is related to its "politicization." Karl Giberson expresses this concern in no uncertain terms, saying, "Until American Evangelicalism rejects the growing cancer of its own politicization, no progress on any meaningful religious front is possible," adding that "I now think of 'American Evangelicalism' as a political and cultural movement—like environmentalists, LGBT, or vegetarians—with a gloss of Christian rhetoric."

In sharp contrast to the perceived combativeness of much of present-day American Evangelicalism, a few of our contributors call for greater openness as the key to a vital future. Peter Enns says, "I see 'openness to the other' as a *pressing challenge* and a

---

3. See Hunter, *Change the World*.

The Future of American Evangelicalism

pressing need for the future of Evangelicalism." He elaborates by calling for four types of openness:

> *Openness to true developments in the intellectual drama of the human species*—genuine, agreed upon, scientific developments need to be accepted for what they are—and not at a distance, but brought into theological and hermeneutical discussions of our faith. To do otherwise is to concede that God himself is outmoded.
>
> *Openness to different ecclesiastical traditions*—in our ever-shrinking world, Evangelicalism cannot afford to be seen as anything other than in serious dialogue with other Christians communions. The global Christian faith must work toward a deep unity in basics amid diversity of various local and ecclesiastical traditions.
>
> *Openness to different expressions of the spiritual journey*—most global citizens claim to adhere to some sort of religious/spiritual practice and faith, and most of them are not American Evangelicals. Evangelicalism must be willing to listen as much as speak, and be willing to have its own traditions examined, and even to learn from those of other faiths and to take their expression of faith seriously.
>
> *Openness to holding to Scripture in a different way*—the recurring tensions over inerrancy within Evangelicalism are fueled by the distance between *a priori* theological expectations about God and how his book should behave, and the non-cooperative details of biblical interpretation. The nature of Scripture is not a closed question, and within Evangelicalism, an invitation to open and safe discussions is sorely needed.

Kyle Roberts likewise envisions "An evangelical Christianity that is open to new movements of God, and yet able to discern truth from error, and justice from injustice."

A Future for American Evangelicalism

A MORE GENEROUS AND KINDER EVANGELICALISM CHARACTERIZED BY HUMILITY

The movement from combativeness to openness will lead to the kinder, more generous, and gentler Evangelicalism that Richard Mouw and Jeannine Brown have invited us to.

As already suggested by John Hawthorne, this movement will be characterized by "honesty and humility" rather than the "posturing and argumentation" that characterizes the combative style. Along the same lines, Kyle Roberts envisions "An evangelical Christianity that embraces the reconciliation message of the gospel" at the same time that it is "self-critical and epistemologically humble."

THE ULTIMATE AUTHORITY OF TRUTH

Coming back full-circle, you may recall my anticipation in the preface to this book that for me to propose that openness needs to be a necessary companion to commitment can easily be misinterpreted as my being "soft on the truth." I hope I have convinced you that this is not the case. My commitment to the openness pole of that important dyad is merely my acknowledgment that I am on a pilgrimage toward a better understanding of Truth, as only God fully understands it, which is far removed from a denial of Truth.

My dream for American Evangelicalism is that evangelicals be characterized by that rare combination of commitment and openness. This dream is seconded most succinctly and eloquently by Kyle Roberts when he envisions "an American Evangelicalism that *seeks and embraces truth*, even when it runs counter to received and cherished interpretations of Scripture and reality."

CAN WE TALK?

By now, you have surely gathered that the search for Truth that I embrace can only be fostered if those evangelicals who are

The Future of American Evangelicalism

characterized by the unusual combination of commitment and openness engage one another in respectful conversation about their agreements and disagreements, thereby completing the triad of commitment, openness, and conversation that is the central theme of this book. Since our beliefs about the issue at hand are deeply informed by our differing particularities, we need to respectfully listen to one another in our communal effort to better understand God's Truth.

But this dream of mine will be all for naught if we do not forsake some old habits. First, as suggested by John Hawthorne, we need to eschew any attempts "to control outcomes" of our ongoing conversations. One cannot set preconditions for the results of our future conversations, for as I say every chance I get, "one cannot predict beforehand the results of a respectful conversation."[4]

We evangelicals also need to do better at creating safe and welcoming spaces for evangelical voices that dare to question some current beliefs and practices. As Karl Giberson suggests, we need to avoid the "silencing of reforming, even prophetic, voices within the evangelical community." Rather, as Giberson adds, "we need to embrace diversity and even controversy; we need to *value* critical voices from within."

It is my hope and fervent prayer that in the days to come, American evangelicals will model that rare triad of commitment, openness, and conversation that I believe must be exemplified if we are to be faithful partners with God in God's project of reconciliation.

---

4. Harold Heie, "Mission," *Respectful Conversation*, 2013 http://www.respectfulconversation.net/mission.

Bibliography

Balmer, Randall. *Thy Kingdom Come: How the Religious Right Distorts Faith and Threatens America*. New York: Basic, 2007.
———. *The Making of Evangelicalism: From Revivalism to Politics and Beyond*. Waco: Baylor University Press, 2010.
———. *Redeemer: The Life of Jimmy Carter*. New York: Basic, 2014.
Barbour, Ian G. *Myths, Models, and Paradigms: A Comparative Study in Science and Religion*. New York: Harper & Row, 1974.
Barrett, Matthew, and Ardel B. Canady, eds. *Four Views on the Historical Adam*. Grand Rapids: Zondervan, 2013.
Bebbington, David W. *Evangelicalism in Modern Britain: A History from the 1730s to the 1980s*. London: Routledge, 1989.
Benne, Robert. *Quality with Soul: How Six Premier Colleges and Universities Keep Faith with Their Religious Traditions*. Grand Rapids: Eerdmans, 2001.
Berger, Peter, and Richard John Neuhaus. *To Empower People: From State to Civil Society*. Washington, DC: American Enterprise Institute, 1996.
Blankenhorn, David, and Jean Bethke Elshtain. *A Call to Civil Society: Why Democracy Needs Moral Truths*. New York: Institute for American Values, 1998.
Bloesch, Donald G. *The Future of Evangelical Christianity: A Call for Unity Amid Diversity*. New York: Doubleday, 1983.
Blum, Peter C. "Yoder's Patience and/with Derrida's *Différence*." In *The New Yoder*, edited by Peter C. Dula and Chris K. Huebner, 106–20. Eugene, OR: Cascade, 2010.
Boyd, Gregory A., and Paul R. Eddy. *Across the Spectrum: Understanding Issues in Evangelical Theology*. Grand Rapids: Baker, 2002.
Burtchaell, James. *The Dying of the Light: The Disengagement of Colleges and Universities from Their Christian Churches*. Grand Rapids: Eerdmans, 1998.
Carpenter, Joel A. *Revive Us Again: The Reawakening of American Fundamentalism*. Oxford: Oxford University Press, 1997.

Bibliography

Coles, Romand. "The Wild Patience of John Howard Yoder: 'Outsiders' and the 'Otherness of the Church.'" In *The New Yoder*, edited by Peter C. Dula and Chris K. Huebner, 216–52. Eugene, OR: Cascade, 2010.

Collins, Francis. *The Language of God: A Scientist Presents Evidence for Belief.* New York: Free Press, 2006.

Collins, Kenneth J. *Power, Politics, and the Fragmentation of Evangelicalism: From the Scopes Trial to the Obama Administration.* Downers Grove, IL: InterVarsity, 2012.

Dayton, Donald W. *Discovering an Evangelical Heritage.* Grand Rapids: Baker Academic, 1976.

Dayton, Donald W., et al. *Rediscovering an Evangelical Heritage: A Tradition and Trajectory of Integrating Piety and Justice.* Grand Rapids: Baker Academic, 2014.

Dayton, Donald W., and Robert K. Johnston, eds. *The Variety of American Evangelicalism.* Chattanooga: University of Tennessee Press, 1991.

Dockery, David S., ed. *The Challenge of Postmodernism.* Grand Rapids: Baker, 2001.

Downing, Crystal L. *How Postmodernism Serves (My) Faith: Questioning Truth in Language, Philosophy, and Art.* Downers Grove, IL: InterVarsity, 2006.

Enns, Peter. *The Evolution of Adam: What the Bible Does and Doesn't Say About Human Origins.* Grand Rapids: Brazos, 2012.

Fea, John. *Was America Founded as a Christian Nation? A Historical Introduction.* Louisville: Westminster John Knox, 2011.

Fitch, David E. *The End of Evangelicalism? Discerning a New Faithfulness for Mission.* Eugene, OR: Cascade, 2011.

Gee, Henry. *The Accidental Species: Misunderstandings of Human Origins.* Chicago: University of Chicago Press, 2013.

Greer, Robert C. *Mapping Postmodernism: A Survey of Christian Options.* Downers Grove, IL: InterVarsity, 2003.

Grenz, Stanley J. *A Primer on Postmodernism.* Grand Rapids: Eerdmans, 1996.

———. *Renewing the Center: Evangelical Theology in a Post-Theological Era.* Grand Rapids: Baker, 2000.

———. *Revisioning Evangelical Theology: A Fresh Agenda for the Twenty-first Century.* Downers Grove, IL: InterVarsity, 1993.

Grundlach, Bradley J. *Process and Providence: The Evolution Question at Princeton, 1845–1929.* Grand Rapids: Eerdmans, 2013.

Hasker, William. *Metaphysics: Constructing a World View.* Contours of Christian Philosophy. Downers Grove, IL: InterVarsity, 1983.

Haynes, Stephen R., ed. *Professing in the Postmodern Academy: Faculty and the Future of Church-Related Colleges.* Waco: Baylor University Press, 2002.

Heie, Harold. "Developing a Christian Perspective on the Nature of Mathematics." In *Teaching as an Act of Faith: Theory and Practice in Church-Related Higher Education*, edited by Arlin A. Migliazzo, 95–116. New York: Fordham University Press, 2002.

Bibliography

———. "Dialogic Discourse: Christian Scholars Engaging the Larger Academy." *Christian Scholar's Review* 37 (2008) 347–56.
———. *Evangelicals on Public Policy Issues: Sustaining a Respectful Political Conversation.* Abilene: Abilene Christian University Press, 2014.
———. *Learning to Listen, Ready to Talk: A Pilgrimage Toward Peacemaking.* New York: iUniverse, 2007.
———. "Mathematics: Freedom within Bounds." In *The Reality of Christian Learning: Strategies for Faith-Discipline Integration*, edited by Harold Heie and David L. Wolfe, 206–30. Grand Rapids: Eerdmans, 1987.
Henry, Carl F. H. *Evangelicals in Search of Identity.* Waco, TX: Word Books, 1976.
Huebner, Chris K. "Patience, Witness, and the Scattered Body of Christ: Yoder and Virilio on Knowledge, Politics, and Speed." In *The New Yoder*, edited by Peter C. Dula and Chris K. Huebner, 121–41. Eugene, OR: Cascade, 2010.
Hunter, James Davison. *American Evangelicalism: Conservative Religion and the Quandary of Modernity.* Piscataway: Rutgers University Press, 1983.
———. *Evangelicalism: The Coming Generation.* Chicago: University of Chicago Press, 1987.
———. *To Change the World: The Irony, Tragedy, and Possibility of Christianity in the Late Modern World.* Oxford: Oxford University Press, 2010.
King, Michael A. "Conversations on Homosexuality as a Quest to Love Enemy Prejudices." In *Mutual Treasure: Seeking Better Ways for Christians and Culture to Converse*, edited by Harold Heie and Michael A. King, 144–60. Telford, PA: Cascadia, 2009.
———, ed. *Stumbling Toward a Genuine Conversation on Homosexuality.* Telford, PA: Cascadia, 2007.
Kinnaman, David. *You Lost Me: Why Young Christians Are Leaving Church . . . and Rethinking Faith.* Grand Rapids: Baker, 2011.
Knitter, Paul F. "A New Way of Being Christian." In *Christian Thought in the Twenty-First Century: Agenda for the Future*, edited by Douglas H. Shantz and Tinu Ruparell, 93–99. Eugene, OR: Cascade, 2012.
Kuhn, Thomas S. *The Structure of Scientific Revolutions.* 2nd ed. Chicago: University of Chicago Press, 1970.
Lamoureux, Denis O. "No Historical Adam: Evolutionary Creation View." In *Four Views on the Historical Adam*, edited by Matthew Barrett and Ardel B. Caneday, 37–65. Grand Rapids: Zondervan, 2013.
Lewis, C. S. *Reflections on the Psalms.* New York: Harcourt, Brace, & World, 1958.
Lints, Richard. *The Fabric of Theology: A Prolegomenon to Evangelical Theology.* Grand Rapids: Eerdmans, 1993.
———, ed. *Renewing the Evangelical Mission.* Grand Rapids: Eerdmans, 2013.
Louis, Ard. "Evangelical Science." In *The Adam Quest: Eleven Scientists Explore the Divine Mystery of Human Origin*, 139–51. Nashville: Nelson, 2013.

Bibliography

Marsden, George M. *Fundamentalism and American Culture*. Oxford: Oxford University Press, 2006.

———. *The Soul of the American University: From Protestant Establishment to Established Nonbelief*. Oxford: Oxford University Press, 1994.

———. *Understanding Fundamentalism and Evangelicalism*. Grand Rapids: Eerdmans, 1991.

McClendon, James W., Jr. *Ethics*. Vol. 1 of *Systematic Theology*. Nashville: Abingdon, 2002.

Monsma, Stephen V. "Called to Be Salt and Light: An Overview." In *Mutual Treasure: Seeking Better Ways for Christians and Culture to Converse*, edited by Harold Heie and Michael A. King, 21–36. Telford, PA: Cascadia, 2009.

———. *Positive Neutrality: Letting Religious Freedom Ring*. Grand Rapids: Baker, 1995.

Monsma, Stephen V., and J. Christopher Soper, eds. *Equal Treatment of Religion in a Pluralistic Society*. Grand Rapids: Eerdmans, 1998.

Naselli, David, and Collin Hansen, eds. *Four Views on the Spectrum of Evangelicalism*. Grand Rapids: Zondervan, 2011.

Noll, Mark A. *The Rise of Evangelicalism: The Age of Edwards, Whitefield, and the Wesleys*. Downers Grove, IL: InterVarsity, 2003.

———, et al., eds. *Evangelicalism: Comparative Studies of Popular Protestantism in North America, the British Isles, and Beyond*. Oxford: Oxford University Press, 1994.

Olson, Roger E. *Reformed and Always Reforming: The Postconservative Approach to Evangelical Theology*. Acadia Studies in Bible and Theology. Grand Rapids: Baker, 2007.

Quebedeaux, Richard. *The Young Evangelicals: Revolution in Orthodoxy*. New York: Harper & Row, 1974.

Rau, Gerald. *Mapping the Origins Debate: Six Models of the Beginning of Everything*. Downers Grove, IL: InterVarsity, 2012.

Schenck, Ken. "The Greatest Common Denominator of Scripture." *Common Denominator* (blog), November 30, 2013 (9:15 a.m.), http://www.networkedblogs.com/RAz2b.

Skillen, James W. *The Good of Politics: A Biblical, Historical, and Contemporary Introduction*. Grand Rapids: Baker, 2014.

———. *Recharging the American Experiment: Principled Pluralism for Genuine Civic Community*. Grand Rapids: Baker, 1994.

Skillen, James W., and Rockne M. McCarthy, eds. *Political Order and the Plural Structure of Society*. Atlanta: Scholars Press, 1991.

Smith, Christian. *American Evangelicalism: Embattled and Thriving*. Chicago: University of Chicago Press, 1998.

Stackhouse, John G., Jr. *Evangelical Futures: A Conversation on Theological Method*. Grand Rapids: Baker, 2000.

———. *Evangelical Landscapes: Facing Critical Issues of the Day*. Grand Rapids: Baker, 2002.

Bibliography

Stafford, Tim. *The Adam Quest: Eleven Scientists Explore the Divine Mystery of Human Origins*. Nashville: Thomas Nelson, 2013.

Thornbury, Gregory Alan. *Recovering Classic Evangelicalism: Applying the Wisdom and Vision of Carl F. H. Henry*. Wheaton, IL: Crossway, 2013.

Vanhoozer, Kevin J. "Lost in Interpretation? Truth, Scripture, and Hermeneutics." *Journal of the Evangelical Theological Society* 48 (2008) 89–114.

Walton, John. "A Historical Adam: Archetypal Creation View." In *Four Views on the Historical Adam*, edited by Matthew Barrett and Ardel B. Caneday, 89–118. Grand Rapids: Zondervan, 2013.

———. "A Rejoinder." In *Four Views on the Historical Adam*, edited by Matthew Barrett and Ardel B. Caneday, 139–41. Grand Rapids: Zondervan, 2013.

Webber, Robert C. *The Younger Evangelicals: Facing the Challenges of the New World*. Grand Rapids: Baker, 2002.

Wells, David F. *No Place for Truth; or, Whatever Happened to Evangelical Theology?* Grand Rapids: Eerdmans, 1993.

Wells, David F., and John D. Woodbridge, eds. *The Evangelicals: What They Believe, Who They Are, Where They Are Changing*. Nashville: Abingdon, 1975.

Westphal, Merold, ed. *Postmodern Philosophy and Christian Thought*. Bloomington: Indiana University Press, 1999.

Wilson, Marvin R. *Our Father Abraham: Jewish Roots of the Christian Faith*. Grand Rapids: Eerdmans, 1989.

Wolfe, David L. *Epistemology: The Justification of Belief*. Downers Grove, IL: InterVarsity, 1982.

Yoder, John Howard. *The Christian Witness to the State*. Harrisonburg, VA: Faith and Life, 1964.

———. "'Patience' as Method in Moral Reasoning: Is an Ethic of Discipleship Absolute?" In *The Wisdom of the Cross: Essays in Honor of John Howard Yoder*, edited by Stanley Hauerwas et al., 24–44. Eugene, OR: Cascade, 2005.

———. *The Politics of Jesus*. Grand Rapids: Eerdmans, 1972.

Zagzebski, Linda Trinkaus. *Epistemic Authority: A Theory of Trust, Authority, and Autonomy in Belief*. Oxford: Oxford University Press, 2012.

Contributors

Vincent Bacote is Associate Professor of Theology and Director of the Center for Applied Christian Ethics at Wheaton College in Wheaton, Illinois. Raised in a National Baptist Church, he has attended a range of denominations between his college years and graduate education and currently attends an Evangelical Free Church, though he often says, "I'm just an evangelical."

Vilma "Nina" Balmaceda is Associate Professor of Political Science and Director of the Center for Scholarship and Global Engagement at Nyack College and the Alliance Theological Seminary in New York. Raised in the Christian and Missionary Alliance Church of Lima, Peru, Nina currently worships at the First Reformed Church of Nyack in New York.

Randall Balmer is Dartmouth Professor in the Arts and Sciences at Dartmouth College, where he is also Chair of the Religion Department and Director of the Society of Fellows. An Episcopal priest, he served as rector of two parishes in Connecticut before moving to Vermont in 2012.

Justin D. Barnard is Associate Dean in the Institute for Intellectual Discipleship and Associate Professor of Philosophy in the Honors Community at Union University in Jackson, Tennessee. Raised in the Christian and Missionary Alliance Church, he has sojourned among the Anglicans and was most recently a member in the Presbyterian Church in America, but he currently attends First Baptist Church in Jackson, Tennessee.

Contributors

Amy E. Black is Associate Professor of Political Science at Wheaton College. She is a member of Immanuel Presbyterian Church (Evangelical Presbyterian Church).

Jeannine Brown is Professor of New Testament at Bethel Seminary in San Diego, California. She spent her youth in the Lutheran Church and since then has been an active participant in baptistic church contexts.

Peter Enns is Abram S. Clemens Professor of Biblical Studies at Eastern University in Saint Davids, Pennsylvania. He has spent ample time as a Lutheran, Nazarene, and Presbyterian, and now has found a home in the Episcopal Church.

John R. Franke is Professor of Missional Theology at Yellowstone Theological Institute in Bozeman, Montana; Professor of Religious Studies and Missiology at the Evangelische Theologische Faculteit in Leuven, Belgium; and General Coordinator of the Gospel and Our Culture Network in North America. He is a member of the First Presbyterian Church of Allentown, Pennsylvania (PCUSA), where he served on the staff as Theologian-in-Residence.

Karl Giberson is Scholar-in-Residence in Science and Religion at Stonehill College in Easton, Massachusetts. Raised in a fundamentalist Baptist parsonage, Karl now attends Saint Chrysostom's Episcopal Church in Quincy, Massachusetts.

John Hawthorne is Professor of Sociology and Chair of the Social Science Division at Spring Arbor University in Spring Arbor, Michigan. He attends Jackson First United Methodist Church, where he makes up one-third of the tenor section in the Chancel Choir.

Christopher M. Hays is a missionary with the "Theological Education Initiative" of United World Mission and a professor of New Testament at the Fundación Universitaria Seminario Bíblico de Colombia in Medellín. His supporting churches range from Evangelical Free to United Methodist, and even though he attends a Baptist church in Colombia, he still considers himself an Anglican.

Contributors

Christine Kim is a PhD candidate in government at Georgetown University, with a research focus on the politics of millennial evangelicals. Her own evangelical upbringing is multi-denominational, for she has attended churches affiliated with the charismatic, Assemblies of God, Presbyterian (PCA), and Christian and Missionary Alliance denominations.

C. Ben Mitchell is Provost and Vice President for Academic Affairs and Graves Professor of Moral Philosophy at Union University in Jackson, Tennessee. He worships at First Baptist Church (SBC) in Jackson.

Richard Mouw is President Emeritus of Fuller Theological Seminary in Pasadena, California. Presently a member of a Presbyterian Church USA congregation, his theological and spiritual commitments are shaped primarily by the kind of Dutch Calvinism associated with the thought of Abraham Kuyper and Herman Bavinck.

Rick Ostrander is Provost and Chief Academic Officer at Cornerstone University in Grand Rapids, Michigan. He grew up in a conservative evangelical home and attended the Moody Bible Institute, completed a PhD at a Catholic university under the tutelage of a Christian Reformed scholar, and currently finds his spiritual home at Thornapple Covenant Church in Grand Rapids.

Wyndy Corbin Reuschling is Professor of Ethics and Theology at Ashland Theological Seminary in Ashland, Ohio. She is an active member of Christ United Methodist Church in Ashland.

Kurt Anders Richardson is Professor of Applied Anthropology in the Graduate Institute of Applied Linguistics in Dallas, where he co-leads the graduate program in Abrahamic Studies. He is also a member of the faculty of theology at McMaster University and an adjunct at Toronto School of Theology. The great-grandson of a Methodist circuit rider, he worships at Highland Park Presbyterian Church in Dallas.

Kyle Roberts is Associate Professor of Public and Missional Theology at United Theological Seminary of the Twin Cities in Saint Paul, Minnesota. He was raised Southern Baptist, then "converted" to the Baptist General Conference, but he now attends Colonial Church, a Congregational church in Edina, Minnesota, where he also currently serves as Theologian-in-Residence.

Sarah Ruden is a freelance writer and a visiting researcher at Brown University and has taught Classics at Harvard, Yale, and the University of Cape Town. Raised a Methodist, she is now a Quaker and lectures with wild ecumenism, including at Catholic educational institutions, the Reformed Church of Poland, and the US Naval Academy.

Dan Russ is Professor of English and former Academic Dean and Director of the Center for Christian Studies at Gordon College. He is a Senior Fellow of the Trinity Forum, a Fellow of the Dallas Institute of Humanities and Culture, and worships at Christ the Redeemer, Anglican Church of North America, in Danvers, Massachusetts.

Mark Sargent currently serves as the provost at Westmont College in Santa Barbara, having previously served as the chief academic officer at Gordon College and Spring Arbor University. Brought up in Baptist and Brethren fellowships, he has since worshipped with Reformed, Free Methodist, and Congregational communities and is currently attending a Presbyterian church.

Corwin E. Smidt is Professor Emeritus of Political Science at Calvin College and a research fellow at the Paul B. Henry Institute for the Study of Christianity and Politics, for which he has served as director. A son of a pastor of the Reformed Church in America, he attends Eastern Avenue Christian Reformed Church.

Ted Williams III has taught political science at Chicago State University and is the chairman of the Social Science Department at Kennedy-King College, one of the City Colleges of Chicago. He is the co-founder of the Way Christian Ministries, a non-denominational church in the city's South Loop neighborhood.

John Wilson is the founding editor of **Books and Culture**, a bimonthly review. The grandson of missionaries to China, he worships with his wife, Wendy, at Faith Evangelical Covenant Church in Wheaton, Illinois.

Molly Worthen is Assistant Professor of History at the University of North Carolina at Chapel Hill. She is not affiliated with any church.

Amos Yong is Professor of Theology and Mission at Fuller Theological Seminary in Pasadena, California. Born to Assemblies of God pastors in Malaysia, he and his parents immigrated to northern California when he was ten years old. He has been a lifelong member of the Assemblies of God.

AUTHORS AND MODERATORS

Rob Barrett is Director of Forums and Scholarship for The Colossian Forum. He holds PhDs in both Applied Physics from Stanford University and Theology from Durham University in England. He worked as a research scientist at IBM for over ten years, as a professor of Old Testament and Hebrew in England, and most recently as a postdoctoral researcher of Old Testament in Göttingen, Germany.

Barrett has numerous publications in fields ranging from biblical studies to physics, data storage technology, and human-computer interaction, and he holds many patents. He also earned degrees from Washington University in Saint Louis and Regent College in Vancouver, British Columbia. His varied background is unified by his longstanding interest in the intersection of faith, Bible, science andtechnology, and culture.

Harold Heie is a Senior Fellow at The Colossian Forum. He previously served as Founding Director of the Center for Christian Studies at Gordon College (now the Center for Faith and Inquiry) and as Vice President for Academic Affairs at Messiah College and Northwestern College in Iowa, after teaching mathematics at Gordon College and The King's College. He holds a PhD in mechanical and aerospace engineering from Princeton University and served as a trustee for the Center for Public Justice and as a Senior Fellow at the Council for Christian Colleges and Universities (CCCU).

Heie's publications have focused on themes related to Christian higher education with an emphasis on the "integration of faith and learning." His website, www.respectfulconversation.net, contains resources to encourage and facilitate forums for respectful conversation regarding important contemporary issues.

Randall Balmer, a prize-winning historian and Emmy Award nominee, earned his PhD from Princeton University and taught as Professor of American Religious History at Columbia University for twenty-seven years before becoming Dartmouth Professor in the Arts and Sciences at Dartmouth College in 2012. He has been a visiting professor at Princeton, Yale, Northwestern, and Emory Universities and in the Columbia University Graduate School of Journalism and Yale Divinity School.

Balmer has published widely in both scholarly journals and in the popular press. His op-ed articles have appeared in newspapers across the country, and he has appeared frequently on network television and on NPR. His book, *Mine Eyes Have Seen the Glory: A Journey into the Evangelical Subculture in America*, was made into an award-winning, three-part documentary for PBS. He wrote and hosted that series as well as a series on creationism and a documentary on Billy Graham. Balmer has lectured around the country in such venues as the Commonwealth Club of California and the Chautauqua Institution and, under the auspices of the State Department, in Austria and Lebanon.